What Scott & Yolanda have don into the art of marital transpare always so consumed with tasks a___ ___, tation for these items to become distractions takes our focus away from being present and self-aware. This self-awareness on both an individual and relational level is where this book treads. It goes to a depth that offers more than just a practical handbook on communication or 5 keys to a successful relationship. This book will challenge you to be present, to dig deeper, and to discover for you and your spouse what your Marital Love Language is. You can be sure your relationship will sing its own harmonious and beautiful dialect after applying the principles outlined in this book.

Joe and Crystal Ayala
Former Marriage Group Leaders

From real commitment to true love to the importance of "me time" the Lupton's are living proof that truly submitting your marriage to God will yield a lifetime of happiness. Sure, each day won't be perfect. However, there is hope if you are willing to put in the work. This book presents itself as an authentic guide to components that make up a healthier and happier marriage. We cannot thank Scott and Yolanda enough for the way they've poured into our marriage. Many of the marriages around us did not survive the pandemic. We knew we needed guidance, community, and real practical actions steps. The Lupton's provided a space for that and it forever changed the dynamics of our marriage. We pray that this book does the same for all the couples who read it.

Andrea and Steven Britton
REALationship Matters eGroup Members

I appreciate Scott and Yolanda's transparency in this book. Sharing their testimony of martials ups and downs is inspiring. I love the candid moments shared for example, when Scott would leave notes in Yolanda's luggage when she would go away. It gives insight into small and practical ways to keep the love alive.

Anita Randall
Elevation eGroup Leader

Great marriages require commitment, grace, communication and a whole lot of Jesus. This all takes time! Be encouraged, stay committed, and remember we are praying for you!
Scott + Yolanda

LOVE TAKES TIME

DR. SCOTT AND YOLANDA LUPTON

SIMS PUBLISHING GROUP

Published by Sims Publishing Group, LLC   Washington, DC, 20003

www.simspublishinggroup.com

Love Takes Time

Except for quotations from Scripture, the quoted ideas expressed in the book are not in all cases exact quotations, as some have been edited for clarity and brevity. In all cases, the author has attempted to maintain the speaker's original intent. In some cases, quoted material for this book was obtained from secondary sources, primarily print media. While every effort was made to ensure the accuracy of these sources, the accuracy cannot be guaranteed. For additions, deletions, corrections, or classifications in future editions of this text, please write Sims Publishing Group, LLC.

Library of congress Cataloging-in-Publication Data

Love Takes Time

Lupton, Scott and Yolanda

p. cm

ISBN 978-1-939774-59-0 (pbk. : alk. paper)

Marriage 2. Dating—Religious life. 3. Conduct of life. 4. Relationships. 5. Coaching

The ESV Global Study Bible®, ESV® Bible

Scriptures marked NIV are from the Holy Bible, New International Version, Copyright © 1973, 1978, 1984 by International Bible Society. Used by permission of Zondervan Publishing House.

Printed in the United States of America.

CONTENTS

A REFLECTION OF MYSELF

For Yolanda and Scott

In your eyes, I see a reflection of myself.
You are my other half, the only one who can make me whole.
I traveled through life, waiting for you to appear,
Not searching, just knowing that God would bring you to me.
And when he placed you in front of me,
I knew right away that you were my destiny.
Our long conversations and similar feelings.
We parallel each other like none before.
You are the other half of me.
The part that I never knew was mission, until you appeared.
The one who understands all my feelings;
Who chases away my fears;
Who helps to disperse my anger.
You celebrate my accomplishments,
And help me learn from my defeats.
You echo me.
You protect me, without hiding me from the world.
We intertwine and become one, and still
maintain our individuality.
In your eyes, I see a reflection of myself.
More beautiful and more loving,
than I could have ever imagined.

By Dr. Angelle Richardson
August 9, 1997

ACKNOWLEDGMENTS

Drs. William and Monica Lupton—Thanks so much for all of your love and encouragement. You have always been there at key moments of our lives. We are so grateful to have such great examples of love, sacrifice and resilience. Love you both so much!

Frank and Velma Vereen—Dad and Mom thank you for showing me longevity and sacrifice in a marriage. Because of you we better understand "for better and for worse" and how faith, prayers and perseverance win in the end. May God continue to bless you both! Love you!

Aunt Evelyn Genrette (Auntie)—You have been more than an aunt to us. You are like a second mom and a joy to be around. We especially appreciate all the fun memories from our vacation shenanigans! We don't think you will ever know the full impact that you have had on our lives. We are grateful for your wisdom, prayers and love!

Elevation Church Marriage Ministry Leaders - Thank you to our Elevation Marriage Care Team Leaders (CTL) and eGroup leaders! We cannot begin to express our appreciation for the volunteer training, support and prayers that you all have provided to us. You have allowed us to be fully who we are and use our God given gifts and talents to serve married couples. Real leadership leaves a legacy, so glad that we get to be a part of something greater as we serve God's Kingdom with all of you. We are definitely stronger together!

REALationship Matters eGroup—What can we say? We are FAMILY!!! Never could we have imagined that what we started in 2020 would become an online community that would connect the way we all did. You all have challenged us as a couple and individually. We are so grateful for the accountability and love we have in this group. We have laughed, cried, prayed and grieved with one another. God truly put us all together for such a time as this. Love you all! Special shout outs to: Brian, Kenya, Ann, Steven, Jermaine, Erika, Cristina, Aaron, Melissa, David R., David C., Shannon, Mama Beth, Roy, Abbey, Max, Renee, Reyna, Chris, Jimmy and Heidi.

Dr. Angelle Richardson—Thank you for making Yolanda say YES so many times this year!!! You are truly your sister's keeper and without your accountability we would have never finished this book. Life happens to all of us but so grateful for this season and can't wait to see what God does in your life next. So grateful for all that you do to serve others and educate the next generation. Wishing you well in all that you do!! Love you!

Aaron Randall—You are one talented man!!! So glad that God connected us. It is true that He gives you what and who you need. Thank you for sharing your gift with us. We are so grateful and know that God had so much more in store for you and Anita!

Jonetta and Orlando Valree—Who could have known that 25 years ago we would all be here? You both are our "Day Ones"! Thank you for always being a couple that exemplifies sacrifice, ambition and humility. We all have dreamt together and built together. You are one of the most down to earth couples we know, and we are so glad that you are a part of our circle of friends who inspire us to strive for GREATER!

BIG Prayer Group—When God's women get together and pray, it is truly a sight to behold!!! You ladies have prayed our family through some of the toughest times in our marriage. We have eaten together, cried, prayed and shared our lives. Seasons, life and addresses change, but prayers are eternal. Thank you, ladies, for always being a source of encouragement and faith!

Pastor Joel and Ylawnda Peebles—City of Praise Family Ministries—While you may not know it, our marriage may not have evolved without the sage advice that we received from your classes many years ago. Thank you both for being an example of a Godly marriage and showing us how to daily walk this out God's way. Jericho was the first church that showed us how to live the scriptures in our lives...we are forever grateful for the time we spent there.

Sims Publishing Group—Last but not least, Dr. Sims. Who could have known that attending a conference would inspire us to finally write this book? It has been a journey and at times we wondered if we would ever finish. Thanks for encouraging Scott to dig deep and for us to tell our story from our unique perspectives. We can truly say we have all grown from this project and it has truly been a labor of love!

DEDICATION

This book is dedicated to our daughters, Cecelia and Alexis. We wanted to leave our legacy of love to you for future generations. We pray that you would have courage and strength to love others, even when it is hard.

Also, to all the couples who have asked us to share our story and lessons learned, we did it! We pray that the wisdom we have shared will empower you to navigate the tough times and grow closer in marriage together. May your marriages last a lifetime.

INTRODUCTION

Commitment, Trust, and the "L" Word

In today's culture of "swipe left, swipe right" dating and finding relationships, we have a tendency to forget that relationships take time to build. One of the shows that we watch for research purposes is *Married at First Sight*. Couples are matched by the show's experts and meet when they stand at the altar. While, this is not for me, some couples actually do make it work, while others crash and burn from the start. One of the key takeaways true of all good relationships is for them to work there has to be a COMMITMENT.

Commitment is a vow to show up and remain. It means to do what we say we are going to do, say what we mean, and mean what we say. It also means when things get hard, don't quit. It does not mean we stay in dangerous and unhealthy situations, but we don't quit just because learning to live with someone else feels uncomfortable or different. This is the reason self-awareness, setting expectations and building a vision as a couple is so valuable. When tough times come, and they will, you have this foundation to keep you committed to one another.

Along with commitment, and underpinning it, is a foundation of TRUST. If you are not committed to the relationship, how can you ask your partner to trust you? People grow and change over time but there should be some core characteristics that remain the same about your personality and relationship. Things like, showing up when you say you will, being a person of integrity, and being dependable and present in the relationship. One of the major trust issues in relationships today revolves around cellphone and social media usage. I have heard stories where relationships end via text message. Some people discover their boyfriends, girlfriends and spouses are having emotional affairs on social media. Emotional affairs are just as painful as physical ones.

When trust is a pillar of your relationship, you are willing to be honest and vulnerable with your partner. This means talking about the hard stuff. We should be mature enough to listen and have empathy for our partner. We believe in one another and trust the process as we build the life we want. We become less selfish. Our relationship smooths out the sharp edges of our character which remain if not for the proximity of the one we love and trust with our very hearts. Now, let's talk about LOVE.

> *Love is patient, love is kind. It does not envy, it does not boast, it is not proud. It does not dishonor others, it is not self-seeking, it is not easily angered, it keeps no record of wrongs. Love does not delight in evil but rejoices with the truth. It always protects, always trusts, always hopes, always perseveres.*

(1 Corinthians 13:4-7, NIV)

The word *love* gets thrown around a lot in our culture. Some would say it is overused and its value is diminished when it is spoken. The Greek language has more than one word for love, describing different types of love. In actuality, there are eight (for more information, go to https://greekcitytimes. com/2021/02/12/8-ancient-greek-words-love/), but four are most commonly discussed. They are: *eros, philia, storgé* and *agape*.

Eros is defined as romantic love. *Philia* is affectionate love normally associated with friendship. *Storgé* is used to describe familial love, which is experienced between children and parents or kinship. The last is *agape* love, a beautiful, unconditional, empathetic, and sacrificial love. It is the kind of love God has for us. It is patient, kind, and it never fails. This is the kind of love that compels us to think of others not just ourselves. It forgives all things and believes all things. This type of love never fails. (1 Corinthians 13:8)

Agape love sounds good until you realize most of us have experienced some type of dysfunction in our childhood or previous relationships. We walk around daily with unprocessed emotions, brokenness and trauma. This makes it hard for us to receive any type of love because we are busy protecting ourselves. Vulnerability is a scary venture, so we remain lonely and settle for a reality show version of the real thing!

The Tenet of Time

Be very careful, then, how you live—not as unwise but as wise, making the most of every opportunity, because the days are evil.

(Ephesians 5:15-16, ESV)

TIME is one of our most precious resources. Unlike money and material things, it is non-renewable. We are all granted the same amount each day. The way we use it determines how successful we will be not only in our relationships but in life. As I mentioned previously, time is required for two people to get to know themselves and one another. Things don't just work out like we tend to believe. Trust, love, and commitment are built by being intentional and spending time with one another. We also need to spend time alone with our own thoughts and feelings to be able to communicate those to our partner.

Marriages also need "Me" and "We" time. What I mean is we need to spend time with ourselves to discover what we need and tend to our own emotional needs. This time can also be spent with gal pals or guy friends. In that vein, we need to be careful of the friends we surround ourselves with, especially when we are married. There are times in marriage when you need someone else's perspective. We are too close to see clearly and with an open mind because we have a stake in the outcome. Having supportive friends and a few mature couples around, willing to be sounding boards, can make a world of difference when handling disagreements. I am grateful to know three married women of various ages who help me gain perspective when Scott and I have trouble seeing eye-to- eye.

One of the most valuable benefits I get from my friends is their perspective of me. All of us have blind spots. We sometimes exhibit behavior we don't see in ourselves but those around us notice all the time. Spending time with people you trust and have built great relationships with over time helps you see your true self and how you are perceived. You can then be honest about areas of self-improvement. These are the people you know have your best interest at heart; friends who have proven they will be there for you when you are at your best or worst. Make sure they love you enough to tell you the truth even when you don't want to hear it.

What if I don't have friends like this in my life? Well, if you are alive you have time to develop these relationships. Sure, studies have shown it is harder for adults to make friends, but it is not impossible. Some of my closest friends have come from unexpected places like college, work, my sorority, church, conferences, and recreational sports teams. Initiating a conversation can start with a smile or a compliment. We are not saying this will happen tomorrow, it may take some *time*.

Spending time with ourselves and others also helps us to communicate better with our spouses during our "We" time. When Scott and I got married one of the things we discussed was me connecting regularly with my friends and family. It meant continuing my girl trips, family reunions, and travel. I encouraged him to do the same. I discovered this made my marriage better over the long term. When I scheduled weekend getaways, Scott wanted to hear about my adventures. Normally, I returned home in a better head space because I had gotten a much-needed break. He, in turn, would find ways to make me feel special while away. He would do things like leave a letter in my luggage for me to discover while unpacking or complete a project around the house I requested him to do while I was gone.

On the other hand, he would learn new things about the kids because they had their dad to themselves. When he went away with his friends, he got a break from the ladies of the house and could do whatever he wanted. Sometimes, I took the kids and went to a relative's house just to give my husband some time alone to decompress and re-center himself. I enjoyed hearing the new insights he discovered about himself and our relationship when he had time to himself.

Communication, Too

Communication is so important in a marriage. We have bumped our heads more than a few times in this area as you will discover in this book. Clear, concise, and effective communication takes time. You have two people from different backgrounds and families trying to convey their perspective in a marriage with no established rules of engagement. Building communication in a marriage is like creating a new language with your spouse. Each marriage develops their own love language and ways they convey love, hurt, pain, frustration, comfort, and forgiveness. All of this takes time.

Why we decided to write this book

At the start of this writing project, Scott and I had been married 24 years. We wrote this book because couples, those who are married or dating, ask us questions about how we have managed to stay in love this long. (By the way, we are still dating, and we actually like each other.) Inevitably, we were asked to share our story and lessons we have learned along the way. We don't deem ourselves "experts" nor do we feel we have seen and done it all. We are merely sharing our experiences in hopes that we can encourage other couples to fight for their relationships.

We have chosen a unique format for this book. Our perspectives are shared in our own voices. You will get both sides of our love story. Our perspectives converge in the chapter summary. There are questions in each section to spark discussion and self-reflection, both as individuals and as a couple. We pray this format will lead to more in-depth communication, understanding, and insight into your relationship. This book was harder to write than we anticipated. We had to recall and re-live the good and the more challenging moments of our marriage. Scott had an especially difficult time describing what he was thinking and feeling at various stages in his life because he was not accustomed to doing so. This book leaves a legacy of COMMITMENT, TRUST and LOVE over TIME in our goal of building a strong and lasting marriage. If in some small way it helps to strengthen your relationship, it was well worth our time and the challenges we faced in writing it.

So…Here we go!

PRE-WE
Family and Relationship Dynamics
Before Our Meeting

What kind relationship did our parents have and what were our relationships with them like?

SCOTT

My name is Scott. I grew up as the youngest of three sons born to William and Cecelia. My father was career military—he served in the U.S. Navy for 28 years. My mother stayed home with us (when we were younger) and worked in the banking industry (when we got older). Due to dad's orders, my family moved every four years. We travelled across the country three times! Because of our frequent moves, I never really formed any true and lasting friendships. I was the perpetual "new kid on the block." The impact of this on my life did not manifest until later.

My parents had a good and loving marriage. They smiled often, were unified in their decisions about the household, and agreed on how they raised their three sons. When dad was home, he would be affectionate with mom in front of us. Little kisses and hugs were a part of their daily communication. Even when they disagreed with each other, neither of them disrespected the other (if they did, it wasn't in front of us). My parents went on date nights and took regular trips together, leaving us boys at home. Camping trips in the summer, Navy football games in the fall and the annual Christmas party at Uncle Cuddy's in Philadelphia were family traditions they treasured.

Deployment often caused my dad to be gone for several months. Mom stayed home and raised three knucklehead boys. During those times she was, essentially, a single mother. Mom had to take us to our football and basketball games, track meets, and other extracurricular activities. In addition, she cooked the meals, paid bills, and managed our household. On many occasions, she must have been ready to kill us because we tested her patience. When frustrated by something we had done, she would say, "Wait until your father gets home." That familiar catchphrase made us self-correct and act right. Dad would bust us up if he found out we were not being respectful of mom's wishes and following her commands. Even with all the demands placed upon her, mom loved, nurtured, and enjoyed time with us. She was the diva!

Absent or present, dad was the head of the house, but mom was no slouch. They were firm but fair. Dad modeled how to treat a woman and care for his family. This was the house in which I was raised. This was my family blueprint.

YOLANDA

And, I am Yolanda, the youngest of 5 girls in my family. I had the vantage point of seeing all the craziness in my parents, Velma and Frank, and older sisters' relationships. By the time I got to high school, I was not very trusting of men due to my upbringing. Being raised by an alcoholic father and watching my older sister's relationship choices, tainted my view of men. There were two sets of daughters in my family. My older sisters are 16, 14

2

and 12 years older, respectively; my sister Selma and I grew up together. We were just one year apart.

My sister Selma seemed to be my father's favorite. I felt the sting of rejection as a child because I was not like Selma. I had my own personality and dreams. Selma was very close with our father, but he could be very critical of decisions that didn't go along with his way. My sister's insecurities drove her to compliance; she made decisions that would please our father. While neither of us wanted the criticism that followed not doing things *his* way, I never feared it. I realized at a very young age that my dad was a hypocrite when it came to the execution of your life's plans. My parents grew up during the civil rights era. I was raised to be an independent thinker, motivated and driven but somehow this only applied to the outside world and not my home. When we were young, my dad often compared us to one another, which made me want to be nothing like either of them. I wasn't like any of my sisters, which was also a bone of contention amongst us. I didn't even look like them which also led to feelings of not belonging.

"I don't think I will ever get married." Famous last words spoken by none other than yours truly. You see, I had broken up with my first love for the last time. As I sat in the kitchen pouring out my heartache to my mother at the tender age of 22, telling her all my plans of single life, career goals and even raising a child by myself, she just shook her head. I had no idea that God was about to give me a major Proverbs 19:21 lesson, "You can make many plans, but the Lord's purpose will prevail." My mom said it this way, "If you want to make God laugh, tell Him your plans."

My mom and dad were not a very affectionate couple. I never saw them touch, kiss or hold hands. My father spent most of his time at work or hanging with his friends on the weekends. My mom worked at night but spent her days and weekends with her daughters. She was the parent who was emotionally available

3

to us. We had a great relationship and, even during my teenage years, I considered her a friend. My mother was a planner and made sure we had not only what we needed but some of what we wanted. She was very practical and smart with money which was impressive for someone with an 8th grade education. My father was a great provider, but he was also a functional alcoholic. He gambled on card games and played the lottery regularly.

What happened in previous relationships?

YOLANDA

James and I met in high school during my sophomore year. He was my first love and became my first heart break. We had been together 4 years between high school and college. He was a part of my friend group in high school, and we were on the track team together. I don't think I really had criteria for what I wanted in a man due to my daddy issues. I just wanted to be loved and accepted.

At some point I decided James was the right guy for me because he was handsome and one of the top runners on the track and field team. As I moved on to college and started discovering who I was outside of my family, I also started feeling boxed in by our relationship. Some hard truths set in. The first was we weren't compatible. I was so busy wanting to be loved, I didn't pay attention to some red flags that were in plain sight. One of which was his mother, who had more influence in our relationship than she should have had.

James was a mama's boy and that was not going to change. Please don't misunderstand, I believe a man should love and treat his mother with respect, but this was a little different. She was enabling him. He was stuck in places he should have outgrown long before. James' father left his mother. His older brother was in jail. He didn't have positive male role models who were

4

in committed relationships. Truthfully, I had not realized that my own parent's relationship was dysfunctional until I went to college.

Also, James and I didn't have the same goals and dreams. I was a big vision kind of girl and he wasn't very motivated because he was comfortable. Finally, I was in college, living on my own, growing, and changing in so many ways. I was discovering who I wanted to be as a woman and loving my freedom. He felt threatened by these same spaces because he was not a part of them. I tried to reassure him that I loved him and still wanted to be there for him, but I came to realize you can't make someone else happy and it wasn't my responsibility to do so.

So, I made the decision to move on...twice. Yep, you heard me right, I ended the relationship but ran back to the well, only to get my heart broken again. There was nothing left for me there; it was gone. I was just prolonging my own agony because I felt bad for James. He would beg me to come back. Sure, he would change for a little while, but eventually go back to doing the same old things. Finally, I had had enough. We tried to be friends but that was a mistake. I came to the realization he used our friendship to keep a "foot in the door."

The summer prior to my final year of college was hard and heartbreaking. We lost our childhood home in a fire and I broke up with the only love I had ever known shortly afterwards. I was tired. I was working two internships and taking a class as I moved towards completing my degree. Additionally, I was working on myself and learning who I was outside of a relationship. It was kind of weird. The whole ordeal with James left me even more distrusting of my ability to be in a long-term relationship. I started to wonder if I was good enough, smart enough, or pretty enough to find someone who would love me for me. The harsh words spoken over me by my father and ex made me wonder if I wanted too much from a relationship. I didn't think I was asking too much. Then again, I was still very young and had had only one boyfriend in my life. At 21, I began to accept the fact that maybe I was not marrying material. I cried, accepting my losses. I found a piece of paper and started to write what really mattered to me in a relationship and put it in my Bible.

Just sitting down to think about what I wanted in a relationship helped me to look at what part I played in the demise of the previous one. I had to tackle questions like, "Why did I take him back so many times? Where did we go wrong? Did I expect too much? What do I need from someone in a relationship?" I honestly did not know. The one thing I did know was I didn't have the energy to drag someone else along while trying to move forward in my life. I was trying to process too much loss.

As if God knew what I needed, I took a girl's trip to Canada that summer and met a nice gentleman from the Islands who was there for a Caribbean festival. He was on "Holiday," as they say, and was enjoying spending time with his family and friends. Paul loved to dance and was very affectionate and fun. I learned he was staying with his cousin in New York. How convenient, since I was living in New Jersey at the time. We saw one another every weekend for the next two months. He treated me like a princess. I had never been with someone who took such care of me. When we went to parties, he always introduced me to his friends like I was a precious piece of art. He lavished me with compliments not just about my looks but shared how he admired my intelligence, independence, and courage to pursue my dreams. He made me feel loved and adored. No man had ever made me feel that way.

Yet, once again, this was not meant to be. His holiday was over, and it was time for Paul to return home. We vowed to stay in touch and write one another. After a few letters, though, I didn't hear from him anymore. His parents and his son back on the island needed his love and attention. I resigned myself to the fact that I had to accept it for what it was—summertime love. Or was it?

Paul had met every need I had written on that paper tucked away in my Bible. Had this been God's way of giving me hope and showing me that there are still some good men out there who want to make a woman feel special and love her in a way that she could give herself fully to him? I had a glimpse of that in Paul but now he was gone. Would I ever feel this way again? Only time would tell.

When back in college at summer's end, I vowed I would start loving myself the way I wanted to be loved. Since I was still working, I would take myself to the movies and have a nice dinner every couple of months. I would buy fresh flowers for myself and put them in a pretty vase in my room. People would ask if my boyfriend bought them for me and I would proudly reply, "Nope, I treated myself." I decided I would not ask a man to do anything for me I was not willing to do for myself. I am the daughter of the King of kings and Lord of lords, which makes me a princess. Royalty does not wait for someone else to tell them who they are, they are born into their status. I am a worthy princess. Now, I just needed to act like one.

I enjoyed time with my sorority sisters and friends. My life was good, and I was finally content with who I was becoming. I was almost finished with my final year of school and looking forward to moving in with my friend Arianna in Northern Virginia after graduation. I had no idea that God was about to disrupt my plans and re-route my destination.

SCOTT

I never really dated until I was in high school for two reasons: I wasn't interested in girls previously and I stayed in the same city for high school. I was not good at long term relationships because I had to move away just when they started to get personal and deeper. Needless to say, I was an awkward

7

boy trying to figure out girls with no prior experience and no personal point of reference. This was a recipe for comedy (or disaster, depending on your take on it). My first girlfriend, Jane, was a member of my peer group in the gifted and talented class. My two older brothers teased me. They felt that all the kids in the gifted and talented program were "nerds". So, they called me a nerd since I was in the program, and they were not.

Jane was the cute nerd girl compliment to my nerd boy status. She and I had much in common and we enjoyed talking on the telephone. Neither one of us could drive at the time, so we were dependent on our parents to drop us off at the mall to see each other. This relationship lasted about three months until she got saved and insisted I do the same. At that time, I was far from being spiritually mature and didn't have a personal relationship with Jesus. Jane's evangelistic efforts were a turnoff. I was annoyed when she asked me about my salvation and if I knew Jesus. She was cool, but pushy. So, I ended the relationship with Jane.

There were other girls I was attracted to in high school, but I had turned my focus to college. I concentrated on the books and extracurricular activities rather than girls. My father had always insisted that my brothers and I stay focused on education. In his opinion, it was the best way to be successful. An education was something nobody could take from you (my dad graduated from high school and immediately enlisted into the Navy). Through the Navy, he was able to earn his Bachelors, Masters, and Doctoral degrees. He accomplished this while black people were fighting for their civil rights in the United States. Plus, I was still in my awkward nerd phase, so I didn't really see myself as a good catch. I wouldn't come out of my shell until college.

After high school, I went straight to college. By this time, I started to realize that I was actually pretty handsome. Girls would approach me and start conversations. Some would point, giggle, and blush when I walked by. What was this? I still felt like nerdy Scott, but I was beginning to get used to this new-found attention. I was starting to find myself. Throughout my time in college, I dated several women, but none of them lasted, none except Stacey.

Stacey and I were in the same year of school. We met at a party and talked more than we danced. She was a nursing major with a beautiful smile. I found her very easy to talk to and we exchanged numbers. In the weeks that followed, Stacey and I talked on the phone and met each other between classes. The more time I spent with her, the closer we got. She told me about her family and the fact that she was only the second person in the family to go to college. I told her about my crazy life and how I moved around so frequently. She said she liked my accent. She was from Mississippi, and to her, I spoke like a "Northerner". Things were going well until I started noticing a trend.

Stacey was always available to meet with me. She con-tacted me multiple times a day, even during class. At the times when I was studying or doing homework, she was hanging out with her girlfriends or trying to be with me. I asked her about her classes and she dismissed the question like it was nothing major. Since we did not have any classes together, I did not know how she was doing. A friend of mine had a class with her and he said that she seemed distracted in class and did not appear to be turning in her assignments. Once again, I asked Stacey how she was performing in her classes and offered to assist her if she needed help. She politely refused. What was going on with her? All of this led to a confrontation.

I finally cornered Stacey and asked her about my observa-tions. She insisted that nothing was wrong. She said that she was disinterested in school at the moment. I could not believe it! She had an opportunity to not only be in college, but also to break generational curses and barriers and be an example to others in her family! Thinking that I was just overreacting, I let it go.

However, her attitude toward academics did not improve. She was more interested in hanging out than going to class.

By the third month into our relationship, I got frustrated with Stacy's behavior. There was a time and a place for everything. Her college years were neither the time nor the place to be unmotivated. There would be time for fun, but there should also be time for studying, performing, and graduating. Stacey simply didn't want to put in the work to succeed. I remember thinking, "She's beautiful, but she's not motivated." That thought preceded my exit. I was over it and felt compelled to move on.

Throughout the remainder of my matriculation through undergraduate school, I went on a few dates, but I did not pursue any real relationships. I had my eyes on the next phase: graduate school. I wanted my Master's degree and more. After obtaining my Bachelor's degree, I immediately enrolled in a Master's degree program. I went from one casual relationship to the next, never really defining what those relationships were. All of them started superficially. I was attracted to one aspect of the woman—a pretty smile, expressive eyes, or intriguing conversation. I never took in the entire person. As time progressed and I had the opportunity to get closer, I saw red flags that gave me pause. I started noticing little quirks that made me say, "She is nice, but she does ..." or "She is pretty, but she is not ..." I referred to it as finding the "Buts." Maybe that's why my relationships never lasted more than three months. My mother noticed this pattern, too, so I consulted her for dating advice.

While speaking with my mother, she told me I was focusing solely on my needs. The moment my needs were not being adequately met, I was ready to move on to the next relationship. I had little experience in working on lasting relationships, so I typically withheld my feelings and vulnerabilities. I stayed on the surface, dealt with the superficial. I figured there was no need to go deeper because I would be gone just as the relationship was moving into a more meaningful phase. I repeated the relationship pattern I developed in my formative years when I moved every four years. Besides, none of the women I dated really challenged me to dig deeper and open up, so I didn't. With that said, my life was about to change drastically and so would my perspective on relationships.

Soon after I graduated with my Master's degree, my mother was diagnosed with cancer. I had just begun my first doctoral program. After learning about her cancer, I started to focus all my non-school related time on being available for her. I regularly drove mom to chemotherapy treatments and helped out more around the house. My two older brothers were already out of school and living on their own. I was the only son still at home. Dad and I took turns helping mom get to her treatments and keeping her positive. As her health deteriorated, I turned my attention inward. The fleeting nature of life caused me to change gears as it related to dealing with my own relationships. Time is a precious commodity you cannot replenish. I realized I needed to make the most of the time I had and be more intentional with my commitments.

I was devastated when my mother passed away from cancer. She and I were close, especially since I returned home for graduate school. I wanted to shut down and mourn. At the same time, I needed to keep my father's hopes up, assist him with responsibilities around the house, and continue in school. This was not the time to zone out. My fraternity brothers were a huge help in this time of grief and need. After mom's funeral, the majority of my free time was split between my father and my frat brothers. I joined the brothers at fraternity parties and began stepping to keep my mind off my mother. In fact, I became one of the step masters of my chapter and we started performing at step shows.

Stepping is a form of rhythmic, percussive dance in which the entire body is used as an instrument. This body instrument produces complex rhythms and sounds through a complex series of footsteps, hand claps, and chants. It is generally performed by Historically Black Greek Letter Organizations as a way of expressing their individuality and creativity. My step team participated in exhibitions and at fraternity functions. We created a routine that was exciting, a real crowd pleaser. Our goal: win the annual Delta Sigma Theta Sorority Step Show at Howard University. The team was ready, and we performed our steps with skill and precision. By the roar of the cheers, we were certain we had won, but it was not to be. The team from Omega Psi Phi won, which shocked both us and the crowd. We felt robbed. We were angry and disappointed.

Finding my Match

YOLANDA

It was Spring of 1995, April to be exact. I was attending my sorority's conference in Crystal City, VA. It was nice to get away for a little while before finals. Graduation was drawing near, and I knew soon we all would go our separate ways. During the awards banquet we decided we had had enough of the pomp and circumstance. Some other sisters mentioned there was a step show over at Howard University in Washington, D.C. We decided to check it out. Well, when we got there, the show had just ended. We saw a group of Kappas heading our way and asked if the show over and who won.

The Kappas we spoke to had just participated in the step show and answered our questions graciously, even though they lost the competition. I will not lie; they were fine and we were bored. So, we invited them back to hang out at our hotel. We wanted to have some company. We could relax and talk. We headed back to the hotel to wait for the guys.

All of us were sitting on the floor and beds, except one guy who decided to sit in the chair by the window. He seemed to

12

be in a very reflective and pensive mood. We were all laughing and having fun, so I thought he was a little standoffish. We went around the room introducing ourselves. Each person stated the season and year we joined our respective Greek organizations.

The guy sitting near the window was named Scott. It just so happened he joined the Kappas in the same season and year that I had joined Sigma Gamma Rho. That gave us some common ground. I engaged him in a conversation which started by me asking why he was sitting by the window and what he was thinking? I wondered if he thought he was too good to sit with us. He indicated there was no room to sit with us. He was still upset after losing the step show. Apparently, the crowd cheered loudest for their team, but they still lost. Changing the subject, I asked if he was in school. He indicated he was. His frat brother made a point of telling me he was in a doctoral program. We started to talk in detail about his graduate program and he told me he was into Computer Science. I was curious if he was one of those nerdy guys who walked around with a pocket protector on their shirt. Of course, he disavowed being, "that guy." We laughed. He asked me about myself. He really wanted to know if I had a 5-year plan. I must admit I was actually surprised and shocked by his question. Most of the guys I had met recently only wanted to talk about themselves. One of his frat brothers thought Scott was being too direct, to which I responded, "I can handle this."

We had a great conversation about our future and all the things we wanted to do when we got out of school. One of which was moving from New Jersey to Virginia with my friend. As the night dragged on into the wee hours of the morning, Scott indicated he needed to head home. Instinctively I grabbed a piece of paper and asked everyone to put their phone numbers on it so we could stay in touch.

What I really wanted was Scott's number. I planned on calling him during the week to continue our conversation. As he left, his frat brother asked him to page him and let him know he arrived home safely. The rest of his guys stayed on our floor and one of the beds. When the pager went off and I knew Scott was home safely, I realized how much I liked him and wanted to get to know him better.

Driving back to New Jersey that Sunday afternoon, I kept wondering if Scott was thinking about me as much as I was thinking and talking about him to my sisters. I had his number in my purse. I had already determined I would call him after my classes on Monday. Meanwhile, on the other side, I wondered if he was feeling the same way about me. The only way to find out was to call.

I remember thinking my classes were so long that day. I just wanted to get home and call Scott. I had so many questions. Eventually, my curiosity motivated me to dial his number. Scott picked up the phone. He seemed surprised I called. I told him I was happy to hear he got home safely. Just so we could get it out of the way, I immediately inquired, "Do you have a girlfriend?" To which he responded, "Do you have a boyfriend?" I chided him, "I asked you first, so you have to answer first." He let me know he was not in a relationship but was sure that I must have several boyfriends in my life. I responded that I was single by choice.

Little did I know this would lead to an all-night conversation. We ended up discussing everything from what kind of car we wanted to drive, career goals and musical interests. Scott was the kind of guy I could talk to about anything. We spoke every night that week until the wee hours of the morning. The phone bills mounted. Our parents fussed and wondered what we were talking about all that time.

To tell you the truth, I knew by Wednesday of that week I was in trouble. Scott at some point over the last three days had started to consume my thoughts and wiggle his way into my heart. I was not a believer in love at first sight. I was never one to fall in love quickly. I was very guarded and here I was acting like one of those women I used to read about in historical romance novels. What was happening to me? I had never felt so connected to a man in such a short amount of time. But I was not ready to confess my feelings just yet. I didn't know if he was feeling the same way. I was excited but hesitant, not prepared for rejection. I played it safe and waited for a sign I could share the secret I held in my heart; I was falling in love with him.

We continued to speak every night. Friday night, after hanging out with his frat brothers, Scott gave me a call. I was lying in bed reading a book. I loved the way he always greeted me by saying something nice like, "Hey Beautiful! How was your day?" He told me that while he was out, he had an epiphany… he was in love with me. This was my sign. I could now reveal that I, too, was in love with him. The question looming between us was now what? I was in New Jersey, and he was living in Maryland. We both were tired of playing games and decided we were ready for and wanted a committed relationship. Despite the distance between us, we were determined to make it work.

Finals were quickly approaching so there would be no time to visit before school ended. At this point I had to really study to pass my Calculus II class or there would be no graduation for me. I had already failed the class twice. Since it was a degree requirement, I had to pass the course, there was no alternative. Good thing I was now dating a Computer Science guy. Only he and God were going to be able to help me pass Calculus II. Scott tutored me over the next two weeks. I passed the class! Now, I needed to figure out how I ended up in a long-distance relationship and what we were going to do to make it work. The adventure began.

SCOTT

On the way back to our cars after the Delta Sigma Theta Step Show, we met a group of Sigma Gamma Rho Sorority sisters on their way to the show. We told them they had missed the show. When they inquired who won, we informed them that we lost, but would win the next show. The sisters were all very pretty. I admit, for a moment, they took my mind off the disappointment of losing. They were from New Jersey and were in town for a conference. We asked where they were staying and they said Crystal City, Virginia, right outside DC. They invited us to hang out at the hotel and we agreed to come along.

I was still upset about losing the show, but my frat brothers insisted I come, too. I complied and when we got there, we all sat down to chat with the sorors (a common term for sorority sisters). The sisters were all seated on the beds and my fraternity brothers took up the other available spaces, so I had to go sit in the chair by the window. I did not want to bring the mood down, so I smiled and spoke. As we went around the room making introductions, I took notice of one particular sister. She introduced herself as Yolanda.

Even though there were numerous conversations in the room, Yolanda and I talked only to each other for most of the night. My first impression was that she was very attractive, friendly and inquisitive. She asked why I was acting aloof, if I was in school and what major I was pursuing? I answered her questions and had a few of my own. I wanted to know her major and what her plans were post-graduation. Sensing something in my manner, my fraternity brothers told me to back off. They reminded me that she had already pledged her sorority and should not be subjected to my "hazing." It was good, though. More intriguing conversation ensued about our individual plans for the future. She stood up to my line of questioning and asked me questions, as well.

I noticed little details about her as we spoke. She was wearing a big Mickey Mouse sleep shirt with black leggings underneath. She had her hair pulled back into a ponytail and she had a dazzling smile. She was smart, witty, determined and serious about her life after graduation. Wow! She was breathtaking!

My eyes started to hurt. I had been wearing my contact lenses for far too long. Plus, it was getting late and I still had to drive back home to Baltimore. I told everyone I had to leave. Upon hearing that, Yolanda grabbed a piece of paper and suggested we all write our names and numbers on it so we could stay in touch. I wrote my information on the paper, bid the sisters farewell, and told my frat brothers I would let them know when I made it home safely.

On the drive home, I put on some loud music to stay alert. My thoughts were on "Ponytail" (I had forgotten Yolanda's name). As I drove down MD Interstate 295, all I could see was her smile. I had not been this interested in a woman in a long time. Who would have thought that a chance meeting would be so significant? The hour-long drive home seemed like only minutes as I replayed our conversation in my mind. She was about to graduate from college and was considering moving from New Jersey to the D.C. area. She was serious about graduating and actually had plans. This woman was thorough! I could have kicked myself. I didn't get her name or number! I had seriously dropped the ball on this one.

When I got home, I contacted my frat brother to let him know I was safe and then went to bed. Sleep did not come easily. My thoughts were racing. I had so many questions. Why didn't I get her number? Why didn't I write down her name? Was she already in a relationship? She had to be. There was no way she could still be single. But what if she wasn't dating anyone? She was so far away. She talked about coming to the DC area after graduation. Was she serious? Oh, what a night! I had to find some answers. I had to know more about Ponytail!

On Sunday, I called my frat brother to ask about the remainder of the evening. He told me he and the other brothers slept in the room. Nothing explicit happened, though. Rather than attempt to drive home tired, they decided to sleep there and leave in the morning. I asked about the conversations they had with the other young ladies then cut to the chase. What had Ponytail said after I left? He reminded me that her name was Yolanda. I asked if he got her phone number because I was interested in contacting her. Though he hadn't, he mentioned that Yolanda kept everyone's contact information. I had missed my chance or, at least, I thought I had.

The next day I received a phone call. It was Yolanda! I could not believe it! God had mercy on me. Yolanda said she was calling to make sure I made it home safely. I couldn't help but smile as I replied, yes. She didn't waste time with casual conversation. She wanted to know if I had a girlfriend. Seriously? I responded by asking if she had a boyfriend (I know, never answer a question with a question). She insisted I answer first. I said I had no girlfriend nor any prospects and asked her to answer my question. I just *knew* she had a boyfriend. From what I saw in her, it would be a miracle if she were single! Yolanda said she was single by choice. She was focused on finishing strong and her upcoming graduation. Halleluiah! I've met a woman who was serious about education. We continued the conversation for hours discussing cars, music, jobs and the things we liked. It was a refreshing and encouraging conversation. This time I wrote down *her* number and said good night.

I found myself thinking more and more about Yolanda. I even missed my exit driving to school because my thoughts were consumed with her. I had never felt this way about a woman in such a short amount of time. In class, I started doodling her name in my notebook. At nights, I couldn't wait to call her to see how her day went. I thoroughly enjoyed hearing her voice, learning more about her, and our discussions. Man, I was acting like a lovesick puppy.

On Friday, I hung out for a few hours with my frat brothers—fellowshipping and talking about nothing in particular. I told them I was tired after a long week and headed home to rest. To be honest, I was more excited to hear Yolanda's voice than hanging with my guys, so I called her when I got home. Was I crazy or whipped, I couldn't decide? Something about Yolanda was so exciting and yet comforting. Was it too soon for love? I was just beginning to know her. I could not deny it, she was taking over my thoughts.

That night Yolanda told me she was having difficulty in Calculus II. She had failed it twice and needed to pass it to get her degree (who would have thought a Business School would have such a strenuous math requirement). I had minored in math in college and was quite proficient in advanced math. I offered to help Yolanda. She graciously accepted.

It was easy to help her because she was so attentive. She was showing me one of her vulnerable areas and I was able to help her. It felt fantastic. Over the course of a couple of weeks, I helped her to pass Calculus II. It proved to be mutually beneficial. It had given me a good reason to call her often and hear her lovely voice. I was falling for this woman, and I hadn't seen it coming.

TIME OUT
What foundational issues shaped our view of ourselves?

YOLANDA

Rejection and self-acceptance played a huge role in how I communicated in my relationships. I wanted my father to see me as someone special, too. I needed him to be emotionally invested in my life. Since he was not, I didn't have a real standard for what I needed and gave my heart to someone that was just as emotionally unstable as my father.

Self-discovery in my college years helped me to figure out what I really needed from a man in a relationship. The psychology classes I took in college gave me the necessary terminology to describe the dysfunction I saw in my family. Being away at college also exposed me to men who were very different from the men in my family and in the neighborhood where I was raised. It fueled my belief that a different kind of love existed, and it was one I wanted to experience.

Dealing with the loss of my childhood home and boyfriend at the same time was devastating and overwhelming. The uncertainty of that moment remains with me today. In both cases there is grief and mourning because you realize your life is forever changed and you can't go back. in hindsight, moving on from James was liberating. However, losing my home in a fire was frightening and very humbling.

SCOTT

Moving every four years in my childhood left me with a lack of permanence. It became increasingly more difficult the older I became because I would meet people who had been around their friends most of their lives. I was the constant new kid. This caused me to wall off my feelings and emotions, which led to my involvement in surface relationships.

Defining who I was and what I wanted began in high school, but it wasn't until college that I fully came into myself. It was the beginning of my self-actualization, as well. College opened me up to the notion that I was not just a nerdy, introverted boy, but becoming a confident and driven man.

Being open and vulnerable, was seldom displayed in a home, where my two brothers and I were more focused on our competitiveness. Team Lupton's playbook did not include lessons on vulnerability and managing our softer side. In contrast, we were taught to be strong and driven. So, it was no surprise that I had difficulty expressing and dealing with vulnerabilities. That was not a "manly" thing to do, so I had no real frame of reference when it came to that.

Lesson Sharing

Lesson One: Reflect—We learn how to be in relationships not only from our own past relationships but also observing those around us. Scott and Yolanda realized their perspectives on relationships were formed early on by their family experiences.

1. How did your childhood and early years shape your perspective of relationships?
2. How has this affected you in your past and currently relationships?

Lesson Two: Relate—Self-discovery and self-awareness are important in determining your needs in a relationship. If we don't have a sense of what we are looking for, then anything will do.

1. Who do I need to be to get the relationship that I desire?
2. What are some things in past relationships that worked?
3. What are personal habits or characteristics have I discovered I need to change?
4. What traits in my current/future partner are most desirable?
5. What am I not willing to tolerate from a partner?

Lesson Three: Reveal—Vulnerability is key to establishing a lasting relationship. It gives us the opportunity to be fully known, while providing a comfortable space to express our love, passions, fears, and insecurities. Be careful not to put up walls. You have to allow others access to your heart so you can be understood and, in turn, can understand others. Guarding our hearts doesn't mean having a heart of stone.

1. Identify some walls you need to tear down to be more accessible to others.
2. What have you previously kept hidden that you might be willing to reveal to a trusted partner?

Final Thoughts on the 'PRE-WE' Chapter

The way you relate to others is often based on your past relationships and experiences. But it doesn't have to be this way. You can choose to grow and change at any time. Be honest with yourself. Think about what you need from a relationship and what you need in a partner. Even though it can be difficult, vulnerability is the key to being known and loved fully. This is communicated in how you relate with, listen to, sacrifice for, and speak with your partner. Take the time to figure out who you are, what you want from a relationship and why you are choosing the person you want to be with. Then, take your time and get to know one another. Deal with the issues from your past relationships so you don't carry them forward, sabotaging your future. Figure out what you want so that you don't waste time with someone who doesn't value you.

DATING
Moving From Me to We

Identify the list of do's and don'ts you upheld during your conversations and/or arguments?

YOLANDA

During the dating phase of our relationship there were some things we realized were key to us remaining a couple. First, we both agreed we needed to be committed to the relationship, which required a foundation of trust. While this is not new advice, we had to discover how to incorporate this principle in our relationship. This was problematic for me. As previously stated in my background, I really didn't know what this would look like since I had "daddy" issues. How could I trust and commit to this man I barely knew and had only engaged with over the phone? On top of that, his longest relationship had been only 3 months; could he truly commit to me? No doubt we were attracted to one another. We had become friends while dating long distance. We not only had a physical attraction, but we were already emotionally involved and committed to one another.

There were so many questions. Another love principle: There are no guarantees. We must be willing to take risks and put our hearts on the line. One of the first serious conversations Scott and I had was about our previous relationships and what role we felt we played in their demise. Many couples we have spoken with think this a taboo topic. This is especially true in our current culture where people have a proclivity to promote a flawless social media persona. There is this sense that we don't have to be vulnerable; we just send our representative to meet a potential partner. Later, much later, they may or may not get to meet our authentic self.

This conversation was a part of our research. The couples who responded helped us understand the mindset we needed to move forward with our relationship. Scott needed reassurance that he could remain in a relationship longer than 3 months. I needed patience to learn to trust that he would remain committed to me for the long haul.

Another key factor that helped establish our commitment during this "Becoming We" phase was our lengthy conversations about expectations in our relationship. We even talked about how we would engage in arguments. This list was called our "Rules of Engagement." We even numbered them.

SCOTT

While dating, Yolanda and I talked a lot about the future. There was no denying our friendship and that we were attracted to each other. Talking was easy and conversations flowed organically. It was indeed a pleasure to talk to someone who was as driven as I! We both committed to being in the relationship, hoping for a long-term one. This mutual decision was both exciting and unnerving. Was this going to last longer than 3 months (Stacey was my longest relationship up to that point and we were together for only 3 months)? Would Yolanda's "buts" get on my nerves? Would I do something to upset her and make her want to leave? I really needed to get a grip! Yet we grew closer and more committed even though we still lived over 120 miles from each other (Yolanda lived in New Jersey, I lived in Maryland).

Communication—with a capital "C"—was the cornerstone of our budding relationship. We talked on the phone for hours almost every day! Early on, we talked about our past relationships and why and how they ended. Having to talk about my old relationships while building a new one seemed odd. I had to open up and be vulnerable. I had to let Yolanda know how I felt about my past girlfriends and how my interactions with them made me feel. I was not accustomed to talking to anyone about my feelings. That was the old Scott, though. I wanted things to be different with Yolanda. I felt I needed to be honest with her. I have to admit it was difficult to show Yolanda my heart, dredge up those old feelings, and allow them to come to the surface. I was used to hiding behind my "representative" and not being the real Scott. As hard as it was to do, I found those conversations endeared me to Yolanda. The reality is being open and honest in a committed relationship has its merits!

In addition to the painful discussions on feelings, Yolanda and I discussed our ideas about family and friends, children, child rearing, time and money management, homes, cars, and careers. It was amazing how much ground we covered in our conversations. During our discussions, we established what we referred to as "rules of engagement" that we would follow in our relationship. This may not be normal, but it is what happens when two, driven intellectuals enter into a relationship!

Our Rules of Engagement
1. **Be Respectful of one another and the relationship**
   a. If it looks wrong to an outsider and can be misconstrued as cheating or stepping out of the relationship, don't do it. Additionally, if you are going to be late or

out longer than expected, be considerate and inform the other person, so they are not worried or unnecessarily anxious.

2. **Fight Fair**
   a. No name calling, no using hands, or throwing objects.
   b. Be honest with one another—get the issue out into the open so you can deal with it.
   c. Avoid generalizations—Scott was the originator of this one. He hated when I said things like, "You always…" or "You never…" As he would tell me frequently, if there is one exception, then it is not true.
   d. No leaving in the middle of an argument. This rule was added because of Yolanda's tendency to leave a discussion and shut down if she felt she wasn't being heard. Yolanda had flashbacks of interactions with her father. He was emotionally unavailable to his family, which usually resulted in his not listening to his daughter's concerns. Yolanda dealt with difficult, emotional discussions with Scott in the same manner. Scott disagreed with this behavior, finding it unproductive. Therefore, this rule was instituted.
   e. Agreeing to disagree as a resolution. For example, people often advise couples, "Don't go to bed angry." We decided there were times when we would have to agree to disagree. We are not always going to agree because we are two different people with very different upbringings and past experiences. Scott did not view this as a viable resolution, initially. Later he realized the benefit of it when we both have different opinions about an issue.
   f. A cooling off or processing time is sometimes needed. Everything may not be resolved in that moment or in that discussion. Sometimes you need a "cooling off" period. We established it would be no more than 48

hours. If that was not enough time, a brief extension would be allowed. In fairness to your partner, though, do not drag it out. These issues are usually serious. They deserve to be addressed further and worked through at a mutually agreed upon time. If the discussion is not continued, the issues may turn into nasty, unhealthy confrontations in the future and result in resentment.

3. **Controlled Alcohol Consumption**
   a. This was a trigger for Yolanda due to a history of alcoholism in her family. She asked Scott to be mindful of his consumption. She had witnessed firsthand the effects of alcohol on the men in her life. She knew how destructive it was not only to the person as well as to those who loved them. She told Scott she didn't want her children to have to deal with the shame and emotional distress which results from having an alcoholic parent.

4. **Money Matters**
   a. Many couples break up due to issues related to money. Both of us agreed that, as hardworking driven individuals who both contribute to the relationship, we would not argue over money. Also, even if one person earned more than the other, we would treat each other as equal partners. All financial decisions would be made together. (More on this later in the marriage section.)

5. **Infidelity**
   a. We had a heart-to-heart and discussed what would be a deal breaker for our relationship. Infidelity was high on both of our lists. It was the one thing we both agreed would be hard to move past. Both of us valued the openness and honesty we were building and were serious about our commitment to each other.

Building Trust

YOLANDA

A week before my graduation, we planned for me to visit Scott in Maryland for our first official date. It was almost a month from the day we met. I was so excited. My nerves, though, started to get the best of me. As I drove the last leg of the trip in solitude, I wondered what Scott would think about me. After all, we had not seen one another since our initial meeting. That had been before we decided to be in a committed relationship. Would he still feel the same about me once we started spending significant face time together?

As I pulled into his neighborhood I was impressed by the beautiful trees and manicured lawns. The houses were not ostentatious but were a far cry from the row homes and urban scenery that I was accustomed to back in New Jersey. I wondered if I was in the right neighborhood. I checked my directions once more and was assured I was heading in the right direction. As I drove down the hill, I saw Dr. William Lupton's house off to the left. My jaw dropped. I thought to myself, "Is this the correct address?"

My gaze was fixed on what was ahead. I got out of the car, locked it, and started walking toward the door. I was tired and hungry. I left home super early that morning since I had not slept well the night before. I rang the doorbell and waited. My stomach was in knots. A few minutes passed and the door opened. Scott stood there in workout shorts and a t-shirt, sweating, fresh off his workout. His shirt was high enough for me to see his toned body. For a moment no words escaped my lips as I admired his physique. All I remember thinking was "Lord, please let this man be for real (among other things that shall remain between me and the good Lord himself)!"

Scott told me to come in and stepped aside as I entered, apologizing for his appearance. He said he decided to do a last-minute workout before I arrived. He led me to the basement. It was kind of like his own apartment within his parent's house. He offered me refreshments, turned on the television, and told me he was going to take a shower so that we could hang out. As I sat on the chair watching him go, I tried to gather my thoughts and get myself together. I dozed off while waiting. When Scott awakened me, he was freshly showered and shaved. Could this man get any more attractive? I wasn't sure how I was going to sit next to him in a car and focus.

Our first date was at TGI Friday's in Towson Mall. We chatted the whole time, retracing old phone conversations and diving into new ones. Scott was very complimentary, saying how beautiful I was and how refreshing it was to be able to hold a conversation with me face-to-face. Scott eagerly served as my tour guide, introducing me to his world and showing me around his hometown. The time went by so fast. Scott was a perfect gentleman the whole day. As night fell on a long day, I was exhausted.

When we got back to the house that night, Scott told me I would be staying in the basement with him. He assured me his father did not mind. The lower level had become a bachelor pad now that his mother was gone. I wasn't used to this, but his dad gave it the okay. Again, I was cautious. Not only was this my first date with Scott but his father was allowing him to have female company sleep over in his room. Velma and Frank would never have allowed me to do this in their house. Also, as my sister Kisha would have said, "What if he is an ax murderer?" Kisha was scared of everything. My gut feeling kept assuring me Scott was safe. Up until this point, Scott had not even tried to kiss me.

We went upstairs to get a snack. I stood in the kitchen waiting for him. Suddenly Scott approached me and asked if he could kiss me. He admitted he had wanted to from the first time he saw me that morning but didn't want to creep me out. I could not believe he was asking for my permission. No other man had ever done that before. What he didn't know is I had wanted him to kiss me all day but didn't want to seem too forward. So, we did, we kissed right there in the kitchen, and it was so-o-o good. After what felt like forever, we gathered the snacks, steadied ourselves, and with one final kiss to my forehead, we headed back downstairs. We watched television for a while, enjoying holding and kissing one another.

I spent the entire weekend with Scott and his father. The pair of them were very entertaining. The love between father and son was strong and evident in their banter and lively discussions. Scott and his father, Dr. William Lupton, were very intelligent and well-spoken on many topics, especially those related to technology. His father was a gracious and fair man with a love for education.

Sunday came and it was time for me to return to New Jersey. I had to prepare for graduation and Scott had school. Neither of us was ready for the sudden separation after such a wonderful weekend. He promised, though, that I would see him on Friday at my graduation. As I kissed Scott goodbye, I knew that this was the beginning of something different, something special and new. This man was not only capturing my heart and mind but my very soul. I was falling in love, and I had no desire to brace myself.

Later that week, Scott joined me in New Jersey for my graduation. I introduced him officially as my boyfriend and he was widely accepted by my sisters and mother. My father would be the challenge. Scott met my father at graduation, but he didn't really speak to him that much. I had asked my older sister, Brenda, if he could stay at her house. My father had not yet given Scott his stamp of approval. Scott did join us at my parent's house for my graduation celebration, though. My parents had a chance to speak with him, but as far as my dad was concerned, the jury was still out.

This was to be a short trip. There was not much alone time because Scott had to return to Maryland the next day. I couldn't wait to see him again. Before he left, we planned several more dates in June. The time passed at record speed.

After Scott left, I was able to speak with my mother. She loved Scott and thought he was a good fit for me. She especially liked that he was patient, not just with me, but with her, as well. Before she passed, Scott had spent time taking care of his mother, who had cancer. When I explained this to my mother, she was forever endeared to him. I got my father's approval through her. Mother has always been the more discerning parent. If Scott was okay with her, he was okay with dad. On his next visit to see me in New Jersey, not only was he allowed to stay at my parent's house but was invited to sleep in the spare bedroom upstairs. What did my mom say to my dad? Whatever it was I owe her my gratitude because my dad is one stubborn guy. I was shocked but relieved at the same time.

In July of 1995, my parents left on vacation to visit family in South Carolina. They had no idea that their youngest daughter had been packing, not for vacation, but to move away. My friend, Arianna, secured an apartment in Northern Virginia and was gracious enough to let me stay with her until I found a job.

Scott came up and helped me move all my necessary items. We managed to fit all I needed in our two cars. I left a letter for my parents explaining that I was moving to start my life. I left New Jersey never again to call it home. I knew my father was going to be angry but being away at college made me realize I needed a change. I wanted—no, I needed—to live life on my terms. I loved my parents. I appreciated everything they had done for me, but I wanted a fresh start and a change of scenery. I knew my mother would understand. She had declared her independence at a young age, too. It was her story from which I drew strength.

After settling into the apartment in Virginia, I called my parents to give them my contact information. I also wanted to know how they were doing. My dad was livid. He refused to speak to me for six months. He said I didn't have his permission to move out. He let me know he would not be helping me with anything. I was on my own. Shortly thereafter, I found a job at *Enterprise Rental Car*. While I had no desire to wash cars in dresses, skirts, and hosiery for the rest of my life, it paid the bills. So, for a time I lived with my friend Arianna, worked full-time, and spent the weekends in Baltimore with Scott. However, this would be a temporary detour.

As the sunny days of summer faded into the cool nights of fall, I realized our living arrangement was not going to work. Arianna was jealous of my relationship with Scott. So, I moved to Baltimore where I found a job working for JCPenney's. I lived with my nephew until he joined the Marines. I was on the move again. This time I moved my stuff into my sorority sister's house. I stayed between her place and Scott's in Baltimore. I enjoyed helping Scott clean the house and cook for his father. Essentially, I was homeless. I was grateful to have an address and a little income, but I needed to find full-time work.

There were times when I could not pay my expenses. I struggled to pay my rent and car insurance and have enough money left for food and gas. More than once, I wanted to throw in the towel and run home to New Jersey. In those moments, I would cry myself to sleep at night. Often Scott just held me close, letting me express my frustrations in the safety of his arms. He reminded me that my father would be happy to see me defeated. My father had been smug, betting on my failure. He thought I would be home within the year.

Scott loaned me money until I could get back on my feet. I didn't want to take it at first, but he insisted. He said if we were going to be together, I needed to trust him to take care of me when things got tough. This was really hard for me. In my former relationships, I took care of others. Although I cared for Scott, I didn't want to depend on him. But I had no choice. Scott was persistent. We were a team. He insisted we operate as a team going forward if we were serious about making our relationship work.

Our relationship was growing stronger every day. Scott was still working on his doctorate degree at the University of Maryland, Baltimore County (UMBC) and I would accompany him to campus when I was not working at the mall. I worked on finding full-time employment and read while Scott completed assignments in the lab. He had such a brilliant mind. I was amazed at his knowledge of computers and technology. Additionally, he had an internship at NASA's Goddard Space Flight Center doing research for his degree. Scott planned an outing for me to see the Hubble Space Telescope while it was being repaired. It was one of our most memorable dates, along with our $5 Baltimore Aquarium nights, and spontaneous wing combo dinners at the end of a demanding week.

As the holidays approached, we made plans. Scott decided to introduce me to his extended family. I had no idea I was the first woman he decided to share with his family. Everyone was wonderful. I suppose I won their approval, as many of them commented that they could tell we loved each other. The year was coming to an end. I was hopeful I would find a full-time job soon and begin the year on a positive note.

In February 1996, I finally got the break I needed. I received an offer for a full-time job with benefits. Yes! The only drawback: it was near DC. I would have to find an apartment in that area if I wanted to avoid the bottlenecks, construction slowdowns, rubberneckers and inconsiderate speedsters which plagued traffic along the Baltimore/DC corridor. Scott was still working on his doctorate. We had grown accustomed to seeing one another regularly. He spent time with me, encouraged me, and shared all he had with me. I had grown used to him picking me up after work, spending weekends exploring the region together and playing board games until the wee hours of the morning. We had fallen into a comfortable rhythm. Neither of us wanted to revert to another, albeit short, distance relationship.

SCOTT

After many long phone conversations, Yolanda and I agreed she would come to Maryland for a real "first date." It was only fair that she come to Maryland first because we had already agreed I would travel to New Jersey for her graduation. We set a date and I gave her directions to my dad's house. On the day she was to arrive, I was a bundle of nerves. What did she look like (her image was starting to fade in my mind)? I thoroughly enjoyed our long conversations, but what would we do once she arrived? Would we have problems talking? Ugh, I needed to get myself together. I decided to work out to relieve my nervous energy. Just my luck, I was all sweaty and nasty when the doorbell rang. Dressed in my raggedy workout clothes and smelling like a locker room, I went to the front door to greet Yolanda.

Yolanda had on a beautiful, form-fitting, black maxi dress. She was every bit as beautiful as I had imagined. I stared at her just a bit too long before finally saying, "Hey! You made it. Please come inside." I was embarrassed because I looked a mess. I led her downstairs into the basement where I was living at the time. "Forgive my appearance," I said and offered her a beverage. She accepted a bottled water. I turned on the television to keep her occupied while I showered. I washed off the nervousness and sweat. I wanted to be presentable to my girlfriend.

We chatted for a while, then went to the Towson Mall to have lunch. We dined at T.G.I. Friday's. The conversation was great, as always, but it was different because I could see her facial expressions. I told her about my favorite coffee shop and used record store across the street from the mall and promised to take her there the next day. It was amazing to have her with me. Finally, I could reach out and touch her. The phone didn't do her justice. My nerves finally subsided, and we got into the

34

groove of talking, recapping past phone calls and sharing our likes and dislikes. I was ecstatic. We were into some of the same things. I felt we were great friends transitioning into a deeper relationship. Normally, I would have been cautious and apprehensive to have such a quick connection with someone. Yolanda was different, special. Slow down, Scott, I thought to myself. Don't freak her out.

After we ate, we went back to my house to relax and watch television. Yolanda had to be tired from her drive, so I didn't want to keep her out too long. When we got back, dad was there. I introduced Yolanda to him, and we chatted a few minutes. Afterwards, we went back to the basement. I turned on the television. It had been a couple of hours since we last ate so we were both a little hungry. We returned upstairs to the kitchen to grab a snack.

I made a snap decision in that moment. I leaned over to Yolanda and asked if I could kiss her. (Look, don't judge me. I was raised to respect women and I didn't want her to think that I was only physically interested in her). We shared our first kiss in the kitchen. I never thought that a first kiss could be so magical. Wow, I'm in trouble, my heart said aloud in my ear. We found some chips and adjourned back downstairs. I kissed Yolanda on the forehead. It was a great end to a perfect day. We settled in and ended up watching each other more than the television.

The rest of the visit went by in a blur. We had such a great time that I did not want it to end. Coffee at my favorite shop, looking for rare Prince CDs in my favorite used record store, and strolling from place to place with Yolanda by my side felt good. We really enjoyed each other's company. Yolanda even got to talk to and spend time with my dad. So cool. Dad was a gracious host. He welcomed her and made her feel at home. I hated when Yolanda said she had to get back to New Jersey to prepare for graduation, but I understood. I was going to attend, so I let that excitement carry me until I was to see her again in New Jersey.

The week dragged on slowly. I was not at all focused at school and looked forward to talking to Yolanda each night. Friday finally came. I drove up to New Jersey for the graduation ceremony. As much as I would have loved to stay and hang out, it was to be a quick trip. I had to get back for classes and my NASA internship. The drive up I-95 North was grueling. I was anxious. My 2 ½ hour drive seemed much longer.

Yolanda's family and sorority sisters came to celebrate her achievement. Yolanda's mother and father were actually pretty nice. Her mother was a sweet woman with a quick wit (Yolanda got it honestly!). Her father was a man of few words. He gave me the customary "side-eye" when Yolanda introduced us. I remember thinking I'd better watch my step with him. At the ceremony, I got the chance to meet Yolanda's four sisters and had a great time. Yolanda and I stayed the night at one of her sisters' house (there was no chance for me to stay the night at her parent's house).

At her sister's place, Yolanda reminded me that since I had been her Calculus tutor which enabled her to pass the course, I had helped her earn her degree. The recollection of that time and her words of appreciation made me feel great. We stayed up talking for a while, but I needed to go to sleep because I had to drive back to Maryland the next day. As quick of trip as it was, at least I had a chance to meet Yolanda's parents, sisters, and more of her sorority sisters. Before leaving, Yolanda and I made plans for her to visit me again. One of her friends was graduating from the University of Virginia and Yolanda promised to stop by on her way.

After she graduated, Yolanda relocated to Northern Virginia to stay with the girlfriend who graduated from University of Virginia, Arianna. Our long-distance relationship became a closer-distance one. This was exciting news. I needed Yolanda. She would prove to be my rock and support as unexpected changes came at home and school.

My brothers and I were worried that after my mother passed, dad would succumb to loneliness and depression and follow her to glory (my dad's father died shortly after grandma passed away). I was glad dad was doing well. He even started dating a woman named Monica (who later become my stepmom). When Monica came into my father's life, my relationship with him changed. I saw a new side of him. We were single men living in a "bachelor's pad." Dad began to relax some of his strict rules, as well.

Yolanda frequently stayed at the house. It was a good thing because the house needed a "woman's touch." When Yolanda visited, she helped cook, clean and even resuscitated the plants that had begun to whither after mom's passing. Dad often commented how much he enjoyed having Yolanda around the house because she was sweet and helpful. It confirmed how much she cared for the both of us.

School started to really aggravate me. The second year of my doctoral program commenced with the stress of preparing for the PhD qualifier exams. It was daunting. My supervising professor did not have tenure in the department. That meant I had to fight for everything I needed. But the worst of it was it left me unsupported as I dealt with being the sole African American man in the program. I know, it sounds like an excuse, but it was fact. The demographic of the doctoral candidates was Asian, Indian, Caucasian, African, and three African Americans, me and two women. The department was not used to dealing with African American men. Interactions with staff and faculty were extremely awkward. Yolanda got an earful as I poured out my frustrations every night when I got home. Thank God she was there to calm me down and speak some sense into me.

The last straw came when I attended a presentation from a major computer special effects company. The focus of my PhD was Computer Graphics, so I was excited about the presentation. I was especially interested in special effects (thanks to the movie, *Terminator 2*). I sat in the front row, paid very close attention to the concepts and information discussed, and asked the first question during the Q&A session. I inquired, "What can I, as a PhD candidate in Graphics, do for you?" Their answer, "Nothing." They employed Computer Science engineers to build the tools and administer the servers on which the tools they used ran. They enlisted students from art schools to do the actual work. I was deflated and confused. Then what was I doing in school? My hard work, frustrations, and hours in the computer lab would not result in the career I envisioned and had spent years preparing for.

Eight straight years spent in college—four years for my Bachelor of Science in Computer Science, two to get my Master of Science in Engineering and Computer Science, and I was two years into a PhD in Computer Science. I was horrified to discover I would not be allowed to do what I really wanted to do? I felt it was all for nothing! My head was pounding, my pulse quickening. What was I going to do? I could finish the PhD program, but then what? I had no work experience other than summer internships. The one thing I really wanted to do had suddenly been ripped from me. I was burnt out, my nerves spent. I was done. Dad would kill me. I started to wonder if getting a PhD was his dream or mine. Right then I wanted to quit school and go to work. Was I being rash and irrational?

I couldn't think straight or focus on anything else. Thank God Yolanda was there to comfort me and remind me that I had already achieved so much. I didn't feel like I had but hearing those words from her was salve on my open wound. I was grateful to have found someone who understood me and knew how to comfort and calm me.

In the days that followed I made the decision to withdraw from the PhD program and pursue a career. Yolanda had finally landed a job with benefits and had already started working. Her job was close to Washington DC. She said it would be advantageous to move closer to her job. I enjoyed having Yolanda close by and did not want to do the long (or short) distance relationship thing, again. So, I planned to join her in the move. My first order of business would be finding a job.

Bridge to Marriage

YOLANDA

While I had recently secured a full-time position, I could not move until I saved some money. For a while I commuted daily from Baltimore to Greenbelt (a few miles outside of DC). Long workdays and driving over an hour each way left me weary. Scott and I had to make some decisions. We had already begun talking about marriage. Scott also wanted to take a break from school. Moving in together was tossed around as an option at least until Scott, too, secured a full-time position. We could combine our savings and, thus, move sooner. We would share the cost of our new place.

I spoke with my mother about moving in with Scott. We discussed how much time would be sufficient to determine if we should move into an engagement. Surprisingly, she revealed that she had lived with my father six months before they were married. So, this was what I decided to do, as well. I told Scott I would stay with him six months and if I was not engaged by that time, I would move out. It is amazing what we find out about our parents when we get older.

In April of 1996, Scott and I moved into our first place. It was a 2-bedroom apartment close to my office and, later, close to his, as well. Having witnessed how unsuccessful my sisters had fared in similar arrangements, I reminded Scott I was committed to living together for 6 months. If we were not engaged by then, I would find my own place.

We began setting up house and learning each other's idiosyncrasies. We had nothing—no furniture, cookware, silverware, dishes…zero, nada. First things first. We needed to at least get the bedroom and kitchen in order. We could furnish the rest of the apartment by purchasing things over time. We decided not to combine our bank accounts until after we were married. Each month we determined who would pay which bills based on our salaries. Decisions were made on everything from chores to a cooking schedule. Conflicts came and we worked through them.

New personality traits also emerged. I realized I was more of a big picture person. I was willing to take a few calculated risks to get where I wanted to go. Yet, I still held back a section of my heart from Scott. Scott liked to play it safe. He was ambitious, driven, and patient. We discovered we enjoyed cooking together. It was a great way to wind down from the day and reconnect with each other.

Then Scott proposed. One evening in the fall of 1996, I was updating my resume in search of another full-time position. I sat at the computer searching job sites. Scott came in from a quick run to the grocery store…or so I thought. Bags rustled in the background as I read through position descriptions. Scott went into the bedroom to take off his shoes and called for me to join him. I remember asking if he could wait a minute as I was in the middle of updating an online resume. "It won't take long," he retorted. So, I relented. When I reached the room, I laid across the bed. I asked about the items we needed from the store, but Scott kept fumbling with his moccasin. Suddenly his face grew serious. He looked into my eyes and said, "Yolanda, will you marry me?" I laughed. "Stop playing around, Scott," I said between chuckles, "I need to get back to work." The next thing I knew he pulled out a box, extended it towards me, stopped messing with his shoe, and was on one knee. As he opened the ring box, I gasped. I could hardly believe this was real. He asked again, "Yolanda, will you marry me?" I held out my hand and he slid the ring on my finger. I jumped off the bed and gave him a big bear hug.

What just transpired? I was so stunned Scott told me I never said, "Yes." He understood my non-verbal response, though. I reminded Scott that I was expecting cereal, bread, and milk. Instead, I got a ring. He needed to cut me some slack. It was a special moment. Scott reassured me of his commitment. I was not going anywhere if he could help it. We were thrilled to call our parents that night, letting them know of our engagement.

Scott and I planned to marry in August of 1997. Immediately after the engagement, we began to plan our wedding. In the meantime, I had another job change and went to work at the American Red Cross in Northern Virginia. The position was contracted, with the potential to work extra hours on the weekends. The timing was perfect and would help us save money for the wedding. Scott and I had less than a year before the big day. We had to have an aggressive savings plan and, as a result, we shut down any extraneous spending. Actually, this was not hard for us. With no outstanding car loans or student loan debt, we were in good shape. We stashed all of Scott's bonus checks and I was paid time and a half for working weekend hours.

Until the wedding expenses were paid, Scott and I stayed close to home. Our entertainment included cooking, eating home-cooked meals, and watching movies. We only ate out on special occasions. The wedding would be held in Philadelphia, Pennsylvania and Scott's Aunt Evelyn assisted us with the planning. She was a lifesaver then and still is. Things were moving forward. We were happy and excited about the next chapter of our lives.

SCOTT

In order to reduce the length of her commute, Yolanda and I decided to move into an apartment closer to DC. We found a nice, two-bedroom spot in Laurel, conveniently located near the Baltimore/Washington Parkway and I-95. We didn't have any furniture, so the move was easy. We brought our clothes with us. It was fun. We started together—just us—and built the life we wanted from ground zero. I had some savings, Yolanda had her paychecks, and off we went. We both learned each other's sense of style and taste in decorating. Since our likes were so similar, it was fairly easy to furnish the apartment. I had one loose end to tie up, telling my dad I left school and was living in the DC area with Yolanda.

Breaking the news to dad about my decision to quit the PhD program was difficult. Dr. William Lupton was a big advocate for education and, to him, education would lead to a good job which in turn would lead to financial security and success. Simple formula, right? The only problem was it didn't necessarily apply to everyone. One evening, I invited dad out to dinner so we could talk. I purposely asked Yolanda not to come. I needed to talk to dad man-to-man. She actually suggested that might be best. The conversation went as I had expected.

Dad questioned everything I said. "What!? Why are you leaving now? You're so close to finishing and becoming the second Dr. Lupton." I explained I wasn't really as close to finishing as he thought. I was also burnt out from 8 solid years of school. Dad didn't buy it. Reluctantly, I had to tell him my plans. I assured him that I wasn't merely becoming a doctoral program drop out. I wanted to embark on the career that I had put on hold for years and I was serious about building a life with Yolanda.

"Is she the reason you're dropping out? Is she pregnant," dad asked? I shot back defensively, "NO! Absolutely not!" Ugh, I knew he would go there once I mentioned Yolanda's name. I assured my dad he had raised me better than that. Furthermore, I had come to realize the pursuit of a PhD was done to please him more than me.

Finally, I stated as boldly as I could, I was an adult. I felt dad should have been proud of my achievements and happy that I found a good woman. I was going to make this change with or without his approval (although, I really wanted it). He relented and saw that I was serious about my plans. He even admitted that he was proud of the man I had become and hoped that I would find success (even though success would be easier with a PhD). Thanks, dad.

Yolanda and I had numerous discussions about our plans and our future. First and foremost, Yolanda stated that this living arrangement would only be good for six months unless we (meaning me) got serious about being engaged. She did not want to be just a "convenience" for me. I understood her point and I was not the kind of guy to do that anyway. My main focus was getting a job. I had to have some cash flowing into my account before buying a ring. How could I be living in an apartment, not contributing as a man should? I was not raised to be a burden on anyone, and I was not going to start now. I had to get in gear and make something happen.

Fortunately, one of my fraternity brothers was working for a nearby technical company. He referred me for a position. It was a win-win situation—I would get a good job and he would get a referral bonus. The job that the company offered me was better than anything I found on my own, so I graciously accepted it. It was the first step in my 20 plus-year career in the high-tech industry. The work was not nearly as intense as my graduate studies or my internships, but it was exciting and paid the bills. What a relief.

As we started getting into the rhythm of living together, that six-month deadline began to creep up on me. Yolanda and I were getting closer and closer, so the thought of marriage was not a scary one. It was making more sense every day. I knew I was in love with Yolanda and had a good job, so what was I waiting for? I had no real excuse to delay further. It was time to act.

One evening, while Yolanda was working on her resume (she had left her job and was actively seeking a new one), I went out for some cereal, milk and bread. However, instead of going to the supermarket, I went to the jewelry store. I had previously scoped out a ring I wanted to get for Yolanda, and I had been saving up money to purchase it. I arrived at the store and told the clerk that I was ready to make the purchase. It was a surreal moment! Am I really doing this—ready to propose to Yolanda? I bought the ring, put it in my pocket, and headed over to Best Buy. I know, it was crazy, but my nerves were a mess. To clear my head, I wandered around the store and picked up some software. Relax Scott. Go home. My mind was all over the place and I asked God to help me get through the next hour.

I went into the bedroom and put the Best Buy bag on the bed. I called Yolanda into the room so I could pop the question. "This is it; here goes everything," I told myself as Yolanda entered the room. She saw the bag on the bed and said, "Best Buy? Why did you go there? Did you get the cereal, milk and bread?" Almost as a reflex, I replied, "No, I forgot." I knelt down beside the bed on one knee. But Yolanda didn't notice. She continued to ask how I managed to forget something as simple as cereal, milk and bread. As she taunted me about my Best Buy "addiction" I said I wanted to ask her something. Yolanda paused and said, "What did you want to ask me?" I pulled out the ring. "Will you marry me?" She stared at me for a second, dumfounded. "What?" I repeated, "Will you marry me?" In disbelief, she said emphatically, "Stop playing!" Then she *noticed* the ring, jumped off the bed and tackled me. She started kissing me and gave me a big hug. I guess that meant yes, though I don't remember her saying it. I *do* remember thinking, "This is really happening. She said yes. I did it. We're engaged!" I couldn't believe how far we'd come. My best friend was now my fian-cée. I took a deep breath and gave my heart permission to beat again.

TIME OUT
What foundational issues shaped our dating experience?

YOLANDA

Uncertainty is a part of life and transition. Moving away from home, finding work in a new city and state can be scary, but no risk, no reward. There are very few things in life that are certain. Learning to manage our emotions amid change is an important skill in life and marriage.

Perseverance/Resilience are the building blocks, helping build confidence so we do not succumb to life's challenges. When we are faced with an obstacle, overcoming it gives us the strength and wisdom needed to tackle bigger issues in the future. My faith is significant. It is the reason I was able to endure so much while establishing myself. It anchored me. I believed there was something better ahead for me.

Transition is the process through which we move forward into our destiny and purpose. Each time we take a step in a new direction we discover new things about ourselves and those around us. Growth requires transition. The best thing we can do for ourselves is to trust the God who created us and the process he is using to develop us. *For we are God's handiwork, created in Christ Jesus to do good works, which God prepared in advance for us to do.* (Ephesians 2:10 NIV)

Overcoming pride and operating in humility help to build intimacy. Your partner should be a safe space for you physically and emotionally. If we can't trust our partners at our most vulnerable moments, then we are not with the right person.

SCOTT

Overcoming mental hang-ups can free us up in our relationships. Many times, these mental hang-ups are borne out of past hurts or insecurities. Work through them with an accountability partner. Consider your spouse, minister, or a professional counselor. The work you put in will prevent you from acting irrationally or unfairly.

Emotional honesty is a key to communication and building trust with your partner. It informs them about boundaries and alerts them to how you are feeling about a given situation or discussion topic.

Facing fears is a part of growing up and maturing. Fears can prevent you from moving forward into what God wants you to do or where God wants you to go. Facing your fears builds confidence and helps you to grow in many different aspects.

Lesson Sharing

Lesson One: Reflect—Yolanda and Scott both had fathers who questioned the stability and validity of their relationship. It can be difficult to contradict and confront family expectations. The intentional, candid conversations they shared about insecurities, difficult decisions, emotional triggers, and daily life challenges provided a foundation for uncomfortable discussions with their parents. Their belief in their relationship was forged through those discussions. Because of this, they both stood up to their families and did what their hearts said do.

1. How much influence do external forces have on your relationship?

2. Has this led to issues in your current relationship or past relationships?

Lesson Two: Relate—Yolanda and Scott both experienced levels of uncertainty and fear in their relationship. Yolanda had to weigh independence versus dependence, job instability and moving to a new region. Scott had to deal with his motivation for leaving school and maintaining a long-term relationship. Nothing is ever certain in life, even when we think we have a fool-proof plan. Fear is based in unanswered questions, unfulfilled expectations, and insecurity. When all of your questions are answered, your expectations are realistic and you are secure in yourself, your goals, and desires, there is no need to fear.

1. What are some fears you have had when starting a new relationship?
2. Did you ever end a relationship prematurely because of the fear that it would not last or be sustainable?
3. What would you do/did you do differently in the next relationship?

Lesson Three: Reveal—Yolanda and Scott came up with some rules of engagement. These rules gave them equal footing in difficult, emotional, and reflective interactions. Once drafted, they had to agree on the rules, noting each person's needs based on past experiences. They also had to be emotionally and physically present and offer grace, when necessary. Individual sacrifices had to be made for the sake of open and honest communication in the relationship.

1. What specific things govern the rules of engagement for your relationship?
2. What would be your deal breakers?
3. Work together to create your own rules of engagement.

Final Thoughts on
'MOVING FROM ME TO WE' Chapter

Truth and commitment are key building blocks in a relationship. Being honest with ourselves and our partners leads to a deeper commitment. If you can't be truthful with your partner you don't need to be with them. Rely on each other and define what your relationship means to you. Take the time to discuss with your partner what things are acceptable in the relationship and what things are not. Have this discussion early on and tweak it as you grow together.

Boundaries are necessary for us and others. Boundaries stop us from running over others and prohibits them from running over us. Relationships need boundaries so there will be a clear understanding between the individuals looking toward building a partnership. The Rules of Engagement became the boundaries by which we governed our personal behavior, the way we chose to communicate and make mutually agreed upon decisions in our relationship. Boundaries are necessary because they provide a foundation on which each person stands up for who or what they are passionate about rather than allow others to dictate that to you.

The Rules of Engagement are not meant to be a shackle. Instead, they help us learn patience and compassion as well as how to make peace and forgive one another. You become more conscious of the concerns of your partner and vice versa. Just like children need structure in their lives to learn and grow, relationships do, as well. Establishing rules of engagement provide a structural foundation by which the couple manages healthy expectations, but the rules should evolve as the individuals grow and the relationship changes.

Make decisions together as a couple. Respect each other and listen to your partner's concerns and suggestions. That will help build trust over time. Pay attention to what your partner is saying so you can understand the context and origin of the concern.

Build healthy and clear communication channels. In doing so, you will begin to hear concerns not complaints which can circumvent future discord.

Flexibility is huge. Yolanda and Scott vouched for the importance of flexibility when engaging in new relationships. Sometimes you will have to accept that no one partner is always right. Pivoting with your partner when things change abruptly or something doesn't work out requires each partner to be supportive, encouraging, and understanding. It is the relationship tango, the dance of life. When you're not able to move with your partner, and you're not able to adjust to sudden changes, friction arises. Life throws us curveballs and things will not always go as planned. The quicker you learn to be flexible and resilient, the better your relationship is going to be. People and relationships evolve over time. Things that worked in the past may not be applicable in the present. Be willing to grow and accept the season your relationship is in, not the one you imagined, or want it to be in. You don't know what awaits on the other side of the trial. You will be a ball of anxiety if you don't learn to manage your stress in unexpected situations. Hang in there; this too shall pass.

Wedding 1997

MARRIAGE
Becoming One is Easier
Said Than Done!

Transition: First 5 years of marriage (1997-2002)

YOLANDA

The Merriam-Webster Dictionary defines transition as 1) the passage from one state, stage, subject, or place to another: change and 2) a movement, development, or evolution from one form, stage, or style to another. I had no idea becoming a wife would not only change my name but challenge me to evolve in ways in which I had no frame of reference before marriage. My marriage changed me mentally, physically, and emotionally. It offered a new way of thinking and being. Honestly, I wish I had had an older, married woman in my life who could have prepared me for the feelings and changes inherent in becoming a wife and mother. Moments with my mother-in-law and Scott's Aunt Evelyn were a huge help, but there was no one close to where we lived, I could learn from every day. I hope sharing my journey will help another woman struggling in her marriage, to shift with more grace and intention. Moving forward...

On August 9, 1997, Scott and I were be married in the chapel of Deliverance Evangelistic Church in Philadelphia. I kept it simple. I had only three bridesmaids, sisters from all walks of my life—my closest sister, Brenda; my work sister, Jonetta; and, my sorority sister, Caryn. Each of them held a special place in my heart. The morning of the wedding, I knew I had made the right choice. They were calm and organized while getting me dressed and ready to walk down the aisle.

The ten months between our engagement and the wedding had flown by. There were preparations, meetings, and decisions to be made. Scott and I lived in Maryland so, instead of seeking out someone to provide pre-marital counseling, we did it ourselves using advise from relationship and marriage books we read together. Especially helpful were *Men are from Mars, Women are from Venus* and *Mars and Venus, Together Forever* by noted relationship counselor and author, John Gray, Ph.D. You see, at this point in our lives, both of us knew God but we were not committed to living for him. However, that would soon change.

As I walked down the aisle and saw Scott standing there, I could hardly believe I was going to become someone's wife. I was nervous and excited at the same time. When I met Scott at the altar and said, "I do," it was one of the best decisions I have ever made. I can say today that I truly didn't understand the journey we were embarking on. I now understand why marriage is supposed to be a lifelong commitment. It takes a lifetime to learn to love another person the way they need to be loved while, at the same time, working through your own issues. The wedding, no matter how perfect, is just the beginning. The real work starts when you get home.

One of the first tasks we did after the wedding was consolidate our finances. We decided to use a 3-account approach to accommodate our independent spirits, while making sure neither of us spent bill money. We chose a bank, opened a joint account, as well as individual ones. All money would be deposited into the joint account, and we would both get an equal allowance to be transferred into our individual accounts. Additionally, spending from the joint account would have to be discussed. We also set a threshold for notification. This plan worked well and helped us save money for our next big goal—buying a house.

Next, Scott and I reviewed our credit cards accounts and determined which ones to keep and which to cancel. Store cards, with higher APRs, were eliminated first. It was too tempting to remain disciplined with sales brochures coming in the mail every week. Those cards were great when we were starting out. At that time, we used them to buy clothes. Now it was time to reevaluate our spending to reach our savings goals. We decided to keep one Mastercard and one Visa, along with our bank debit cards. All extraneous spending—for CDs, movies, expensive dining out, impulse buying sprees—was cut altogether. We set a goal to move out in a year. Until then we kept life simple and watched the budget. It worked with the wedding. I was confident we could do it again.

Our marriage was starting out great. Then, suddenly, I began feeling sad and couldn't pinpoint why. For instance, while changing my name on my credit cards one afternoon, I started crying. Scott and I had discussed candidly me assuming his last name. We decided I would shift my maiden name to my middle name so I could preserve that part of me. Still, I could not help feeling like I was becoming someone else. Subconsciously, a part of me was grieving the loss of the "old" Yolanda. I didn't want to totally lose my identity by becoming Scott's wife, but it felt like exactly what was happening.

We both discussed wanting to retain our individuality as we became Team Lupton. This would help us maintain a level of autonomy within our relationship. For me, it meant continuing to spend time with my family, friends and sorority sisters for much needed girl time and healthy connections outside of our marriage. Scott, too, was there cheering me on as I continued to pursue my certification and career goals.

Over the next year, Scott and I became avid researchers, spending hours on end looking for our new neighborhood and home. We discussed the features we both wanted in a house. The internet served as our digital realtor, aiding us in discovering potential counties and developments to visit. I read tons of resources on buying a new house and how to get the best financing. It was an exciting but stressful time. Scott and I were working full-time and house-hunting on the weekends. We were young and determined. There were times when we would walk into places and be ignored until we wrote down our incomes.

We finally decided on a neighborhood in Prince George's County, MD. We encountered a builder who was closing out a neighborhood where we initially wanted to build a home. We sought his services but, when the builder decided to try to intimidate me into using one of his loan officers (we had already obtained financing on our own at a better rate), I told him we would continue our search. It was kind of funny. Scott left for work one morning and when he came back that evening, I told him we were no longer building a house. I can still remember his face when I broke the news to him and explained what happened. He called the builder the next day. The builder tried to pull the same stunt with him, so we started to comb the market again.

The ordeal with the builder prompted us to hire a realtor. She researched homes for sale in our chosen neighborhood. The first day out we found the house that would become our new home. It was a brand, new listing. It was the second house we toured that day. From the moment we entered the door, it felt like the house we were supposed to buy. I let Scott know right away that it was *the one*. The next day we put a contract on the house and within a week it was accepted. We closed on our new home a little over a year after our wedding and shortly after our first anniversary. Whew! What a ride the last two years had been!

Scott and I were trying to find our rhythm living together as newlyweds. Although we had already lived together before getting married, we needed to recalibrate. Things really do change after you get married. For the most part things were going well, but we were definitely in a period of adjustment. In the first couple of years of marriage, I realized my husband did not know how to comfort me. When I was sick, instead of looking to Scott to care for me, I wanted to go home to my mom. Scott didn't understand that sometimes I needed him to help me. He was used to the strong, independent woman he fell in love with and married. Just because I was strong didn't mean I never felt weak or needy.

In *Mars and Venus Collide* by Dr. John Gray, PhD helps readers improve their understanding of how men and women cope with stress.

> *"The responses to stress are very different on Mars and Venus. Men tend to shift gears, disengage, and forget their problems, while women are compelled to connect, ask questions, and share problems." (pg.33)*

> *"Women's brains are designed to consider and anticipate the emotions, sensitivities and needs of others. Men, on the other hand are more acutely aware of their own needs, or at least their needs for achieving the goal at hand." (p. 36)*

In general, we tend to think others will respond to situations the way we do. I found out very early on in our marriage that is not the case. Women are socialized and designed with deep emotional connections. As stated above, my new husband was wired differently. I needed to adjust. I was grateful I had retained relationships with many of my girlfriends. They helped me talk through my issues and I only brought back to Scott what had been filtered and processed. I appreciated their honesty and candor. I have often admitted to them that they are the reason I am still married today.

The bigger issue, though, was learning to ask for help and not assume Scott knew what I needed. This seemed like a small task, yet I was afraid to be vulnerable and let my guard down completely. I was fiercely independent. What if Scott disappointed me? What if my father's words were true? My own internal voice sounded much like my father's, "You are lazy, your sister is better than you and you're not enough." I repeatedly replayed my father's degrading words, "Your dreams are too big and so is your mouth; no one will ever marry you." They haunted me. I was clearly still having problems trusting Scott with my heart and letting go of those insecurities from my childhood.

And yet, here I was. My actions were already speaking louder than those words. My father seemed not to be deterred in his opinion of me. Throughout my engagement and now into my marriage, my father refused to come to visit us. He never came to the apartment or our new home once we were married. My mother, ever supportive, visited both places with the help of my sisters. But my father, as stubborn as ever, would not come. It felt like I was being penalized for not following his plan for my life. It stung. The hurt and rejection I felt once again caused me to project my fears and insecurities onto my undeserving husband.

I started seeking what my father could not give me from my husband. I would get into arguments with Scott to see if he would chase me and offer to indulge me to prove he really loved me. It was childish and I knew it. My fear of rejection left me broken and I acted out in irrational ways. Scott's presence made me confront all the scary places in my heart I thought were healed. I realized, though, they had only been quarantined off.

In the summer of 1999, I was going around doing my normal activities when I started feeling extra tired. Fatigue was merely a symptom of something else. I found out I was pregnant with our first daughter, Cecelia. Scott was ecstatic (after he got over having to wait through the weekend to get the test results). However, I had mixed feelings. I was scared because, truth be told, I was still learning how to be a wife. Now, I was going to be a mother. While I was excited that we were able to get pregnant, there were so many unknowns going through my mind. What impact would the baby have on our new marriage? Would we be good parents? Scarier for me was how I was going to push this baby out?! So, while Scott was rejoicing, I was trying to get my thoughts together before I worked myself into a tizzy and started experiencing heart palpitations.

Cecelia (Cece) was born in February of 2000. She was so beautiful. I was overwhelmed with love for her from the start. Scott and I were financially stable, so I was able to stay at home for a little over 3 months and bond with our newborn daughter. That time was such a blessing for me. While I had taken care of other people's children since my teenage years, nothing could prepare me for full-time parenthood—not pets, babysitting, or being an auntie. (Sorry to all of you fur parents out there.)

So much had to change. I needed to think differently, work efficiently, and learn to manage my days to get everything done. The first two weeks were not bad. My mom and aunt came to stay with me and helped around the house. Cece's birth was the impetus to finally get my father to visit me for the first time since I moved to Maryland. Grandbabies seem to hold some magical powers over their grandparents that their children seem unable to wield! My mom stayed one week, and my aunt stayed an additional one. Once my aunt left, I was on my own.

Honestly, I was just happy I could take a shower before Scott came home from work in the evenings. Everything started to revolve around the new member of our family. Our relationship had to change to accommodate this new person; her birth ushered in a new family dynamic. Gone were the days of lying-in bed until I felt like getting up, reading, or chatting with Scott before falling asleep. There seemed to be less time for me. There was also less time to connect with Scott.

We were both juggling work, sleep deprivation, daycare drop offs and pick-ups. If that was not enough to overwhelm us, when I returned to work, the position I had held was no longer available due to a contractual change. I would be required to learn a new job. I had to put training and schedule adjustments on my already full plate.

I am amazed I made it through that first year with my brain still intact. I think God tricks people into becoming parents. Parenthood looks like pure bliss and so much fun. You are enticed by those cute baby gummy smiles, squishy soft cheeks, and sweet snuggles. I believe the Lord bestows a special grace upon parents because it felt like I was on autopilot most of the time. I just remember feeling exhausted.

Being a parent is very rewarding, but it is also taxing on a relationship. Since our parents and relatives were not in the immediate area, there would not be spontaneous date or movie nights out. Scott and I were unable to talk until after I nursed the baby. Most of the time, I fell asleep while nursing. My husband would start a conversation and soon realize I was not responding. We needed to find a different way to communicate and spend time with one another or before long we were going to have some serious problems. We decided we needed to work out a plan to get us back on track. We started a rotating sleep schedule on the weekends. We also thought through how we might schedule time for quality re-connections during the week.

As Cece approached her second birthday, I felt God calling me back to church. Scott and I had finally decided to look for a church in our local area. It took us awhile but, at the invitation of a co-worker, we visited and started attending Jericho City of Praise in Landover, Maryland. I had no idea what to expect. It was a non-denominational church. I had attended a small Lutheran church as a teen and my mom's Baptist church as a child. Scott had grown up on Naval bases and was exposed to non-denominational churches, which leaned more towards Catholicism. We were trying to find some middle ground. Jericho was a good fit.

It felt good to attend church again. I didn't realize how alone I had been feeling. I missed the fellowship and community that comes with regular church attendance. I love the Black church mothers who smile at you, read your facial expressions and spirit, and encourage you when you are tired. They help you understand motherhood. They know it is exhausting and urge young mothers to give yourself a break. They helped me understand that even the best moms are not perfect. All mothers are flawed. Their sage advice to young mothers was to give yourself grace. Jericho became a place of refreshing. I now had the freedom to discover God in my own way as an adult, wife, and mother.

Scott and I signed up for a Wednesday night marriage series on God's expectations of marriage. For the first time I was going to receive information on what marriage is supposed to look like from a biblical point of view. The teaching forever changed my expectations of my husband and myself, too. Pastor Joel Peebles and his wife, spent weeks discussing how women and men process their thoughts, actions and the events of their lives. They stressed that God has to be at the center of a marriage or things will go off track. The couples discussed the meaning of submission, which was a distasteful word to me. Submission didn't mean I had to be a doormat for my husband. I was introduced to love languages. I learned to give to others what they need not what I need. They gave us verbiage for some of the common issues we were facing and suggestions on resolving them. For the first time in my life, I was seeing marriage from a different perspective. I envisioned the kind of marriage I wanted and, also, the kind of parent I wanted to be.

I sought God's heart for marriage in other resources and conferences so I could apply the principles to my marriage. I had no examples in my family of Godly marriages. Applying those marriage principles was not easy for me. This was one of the reasons I had not want to get married. However, I also believe it was the reason God moved me out of New Jersey before I was married. Attending church, reading God's word and other Christian material, and listening to messages our pastor preached led me to the first major step I needed to take on my journey to freedom and forgiveness. If I was ever going to move beyond my past, I had to forgive my dad. Unforgiveness was at the root of my insecurities.

I have to be honest with you; this was the last thing I wanted to do. But to heal and move forward, I had to rip the Band-Aid off and deal with my relationship with my dad. My dad avoids hard conversations at all cost. I knew this going in which made it more of a struggle. My dad was still drinking at the time, and I could not understand why God wanted me to do this. I was 28 years old and I was still upset my dad had not visited me the first 5 years after I moved away from home; never really said he loved me; or, acknowledged anything I had accomplished since graduation. After weighing the options, I decided to write a letter, filling the pages with my pain. I cried the entire time I was writing. My father never responded, not a word. It did not matter. Finally, I felt free.

SCOTT

Yolanda and I decided to get married in Philadelphia. Her family lived in nearby Trenton, New Jersey, my extended family lived in Philadelphia, and my cousin, Clement, ministered at a church in Philadelphia. Clement cheerfully agreed to officiate the ceremony and Aunt Evelyn (Auntie) volunteered to be our local Philadelphia wedding planner. We were set. Yolanda and I made frequent trips up to Philly for wedding planning meetings and to visit family. On one such trip, my car quit on me. We were stranded in Northern Maryland and had to ask my dad to rescue us. Just what we needed, an unexpected expense while making wedding plans and financing them ourselves (Yolanda and I agreed to fund the wedding). We needed two vehicles, so I had to get a new car. Ugh, I needed more money.

After purchasing another car, Yolanda and I focused on the wedding costs. Fortunately, Auntie was brilliant at finding great deals. She negotiated the cost of the wedding cake, reception venue, photographer, a custom-painted cake topper, tuxedo rentals for my groomsmen and more. I already owned a tuxedo (since I often attended black tie events for my fraternity) so we saved that cost. Yolanda worked extra hours and I received a few bonuses, all of which were used for wedding expenses. Our dads helped, too. Mine agreed to pay for the rehearsal dinner and Yolanda's offered his Lincoln Town Car so we wouldn't have to pay for a limousine. Things were working out for us.

On August 9, 1997, Yolanda and I were married. The day seemed to move on fast forward. My oldest brother Mike was my best man. My other brother Steve and step-brother Ian were my groomsmen. All of us arrived at the church early. It was amazing to see things happening according to plan. I was a little nervous. Planning the wedding was one thing but now we were in the middle of it. We were really doing this.

I was deep in thought with an uneasy look on my face. My cousin Clement saw the look on my face and told me he felt that Yolanda and I would be blessed and have a great marriage. His reassurance helped to ease my nerves. But my older brother Steve was visibly shaking. He said he was very nervous, but I didn't understand why. I was getting married not him. I guess he was just nervous being this close to a wedding, no matter who was getting married.

I stood there at the altar as time stood still. All day the speed of the events was dizzying; now it switched to super, slow motion.

Yolanda was escorted down the aisle by her father. She was breathtaking. The A-line silhouette of her dress complimented her shape elegantly. Her hair was in an up-do with a few curls wrapping her face. I could see her bright eyes and pretty smile even through the veil. My stomach was full of butterflies and my throat was dry. Was I nervous or just excited? I don't know. When Yolanda met me at the altar, my heart was full, but my knees were weak. I put on my best grin and looked deeply into her eyes. We made it.

As if he could sense the excitement and anticipation, Cousin Clement started the wedding ceremony with style and clarity. What did he say? What did I say? I blinked and he said I could kiss my bride. And kiss we did. Once again, I felt weak in the knees. We did it, yes! The rest of the day sped up again. I could not remember what had happened, I just hoped I didn't mess up anything.

Life for us changed dramatically after we got married. Yes, we went back to the apartment and to our regularly scheduled lives, but we also faced many differences. One change was in how we managed our finances. Where we once had separate accounts and managed finances independently, we consolidated our finances into three checking accounts at the same bank: a joint account from which we paid all the bills, and individual accounts for the both of us. With this setup, we would deposit our paychecks into the joint account and transfer our "allowance" into our separate accounts. All minor expenses (e.g. coffee, lunches, minor purchases under $100) came from our individual accounts. I actually liked this change because it simplified how we paid bills. It also freed me up to make small purchases without touching our household money. This worked well within our rules of engagement.

Organizing our finances helped us with an even bigger change: buying a house. Renting an apartment was fine, but we really wanted a house. This was the biggest step in our marriage so far. Yolanda had her criteria. She insisted on a large kitchen, master bedroom suite, and a large tub. I liked her ideas and had a few of my own. I wanted a two-car garage, finished basement, and deck. Yolanda was skilled in researching and locating great neighborhoods. We decided Bowie was the best area for us. It was in a great location and close to our jobs. Once we found our target neighborhood, we found a lot that was open for new construction. We met with the builder and made some progress toward building a house that met our needs.

The representative, however, made an incorrect assumption that enraged Yolanda, which led to an abrupt about face. I didn't know about the builder's blunder. I went to work one day feeling like we were close to building a house. When I arrived home that evening, Yolanda said she was done with the builder. Huh? What? She explained to me the builder's attempt to strong-arm us into using his lender. We had done our homework. We procured funds with our credit union which no other lender could beat or even match. To top it off, he disrespected Yolanda by insulting her, suggesting her age and lack of home buying experience was the problem. Upon hearing this, I was done, too. No deal. Back to the drawing board.

Fortunately, God was smiling on us. There were a few houses in the same neighborhood for sale. After just two visits, we found our house. We put a contract on it immediately. With a note of concern, my dad questioned our decision. "You're buying a single-family home as your first house? Can you kids afford it?" I told him, "Yes, we're good, Dad."

Funny, our two-bedroom apartment seemed well furnished until we moved into our new, single-family home. The furniture from the apartment was sparse in our spacious surroundings. So, Yolanda and I had to buy more furnishings. Fortunately, we were in no rush. We had the essential rooms—our bedroom, kitchen, and family room—pretty much covered. We had a futon and some air mattresses if we needed to make space for guests.

Taking the plunge and getting a single-family home meant Yolanda and I could "grow into" the house and not worry about moving to a larger space once we had children. Just over a year after getting married, we moved into our home.

Living together in the house posed new challenges for us. When we were unmarried living in the apartment, we had a comfortable rhythm. After marriage and moving into the house, we had to adjust our routine. One area in which I had difficulty was comforting Yolanda. Since I grew up in a house with guys, we never really had to deal with deep emotions. If we got into an argument, or if someone got upset, we would argue for a while, resolve it, and get over it. Nothing deep was said. However, living with Yolanda, I had to change my mindset and learn to speak more from the heart. I also had to learn to listen intently. I needed to *hear* what Yolanda said but also what was not spoken. Quick, knee-jerk responses were not good. Quietly and intently listening so Yolanda could feel she was being heard was essential. Thanks to the classic book, *Men are from Mars and Women are from Venus* by Dr. John Gray, I understood how my communication style (or lack thereof) was *heard* by Yolanda. Dr. Gray's books helped refine how I communicated with my wife. I learned how to not just hear Yolanda speak, but actively listen to her to decipher what was really bothering her. This skill of active and intentional listening took years to hone, and I am still learning today.

Yolanda and I amassed a library of books that spoke on communication, love languages, relationships, and conflict resolution, including more of Dr. John Gray's *Mars and Venus* titles. We took time to read many of the books together. Communicating and listening are lifelong skills we never really mastered. They are ever evolving because, over time, you and your significant other change and may have different needs. Good thing I started improving my communication skills early in our marriage. It helped me with the next big thing in our lives - parenthood.

About eight months after moving into the house, Yolanda and I were finally settled. We got into a new rhythm and were acclimated to the neighborhood and our commute. We even started to get back into our Greek Lettered Organizations. Yolanda was stepping with her sorority again. As we got used to this new routine, Yolanda started feeling fatigued rather easily and needed frequent naps. She was still stepping, so at first, we attributed these feelings to her busy schedule. She continued to get increasingly tired, so Yolanda decided to visit her doctor one Friday afternoon. While at her visit, Yolanda's doctor ran a routine pregnancy test as part of her investigation into the cause of the fatigue. The doctor offered to let Yolanda know that day, but Yolanda told her that she could wait until Monday to get the results. Yolanda needed to get to step practice and was focused on her step routine.

When I heard about this, I got a little upset. I asked, "Why didn't you just find out that day? Why wait?" Yolanda responded, "Well, if I'm pregnant on Friday, I'll be pregnant on Monday." Ugh! Come on, this was important news. Was Yolanda in denial, or was she just being a diva? Either way, we had to wait until Monday to hear that Yolanda was, indeed, pregnant. Oh wow! We were going to be parents.

Just over one year in the house, we welcomed our first daughter, Cecelia. I love Yolanda but I now discovered another type of love—the love for a child. The first time I held Cecelia, I was both fascinated and scared. I was a dad. Oh my God! Not only did I have a lovely wife, but I also had a child. We would be responsible for loving, raising, caring for, feeding, educating, and mentoring another person. I wondered and worried what kind of dad I would be and how we would raise her. I did not want to mess things up with my daughter. I questioned myself. The magnitude of it all left me terrified.

Having a child dramatically changed how Yolanda and I functioned as a married couple. We had to adjust to a new sleep schedule, buy new clothes and furniture. We were grateful for the many relatives and co-workers who showered us with gifts for the baby. Yet, we still needed a few additional things in order to care for this little person who was completely dependent upon us. We developed a tag-team approach with Cecelia. Paternity leave offered far less time off than maternity leave, so I had to return to work. Yolanda was home all day with the baby, so when I got home, I would tag her out so that she could rest and get some personal time. I changed diapers, fed Cecelia, cleaned her up and rocked her to sleep. I had been guilty of playing with her late at night while she was in the womb, so, Cecelia tended to be wide awake at that time. Yolanda reminded me that I started this pattern, so it would be my responsibility to care for her late in the evening after she was born. Okay, I deserved that one, so I acquiesced.

When Cecelia was a little over a year old, the United States of America was attacked. The events of 9/11 shook me to my core. How could the United States be attacked right in its own land? Never in my life had I felt so vulnerable and unprotected. I was a Navy brat, a term that is commonly used to describe a person whose parent or parents served in the United States Navy. For most of my life I had been around sailors. Yet, I never really thought about what it meant for people to risk their lives in defense of our country. I found a new respect for those service men and women.

I was working in Northern Virginia when the attacks began. For a while, I was stranded because the bridges from Northern Virginia into Washington, DC were closed for security purposes. Yolanda was working in Northern Virginia, as well. When she was told to evacuate her building, she came to my office. Cecelia was at a home day care in Maryland, and we could not get to her. Fortunately, the day care provider understood our dilemma, so she agreed to keep Cecelia until we were able to get back to her. My oldest brother Mike worked in the World Trade Center in New York City. Phone lines in the Northeast were flooded with people like me trying to get a status report on their loved ones. As a result, I could not immediately reach my brother to ensure his safety. I was jittery and trying not to panic. I was grateful that at least Yolanda was with me in the office. But my baby was a few miles away and my brother at risk. I cried out, "Lord, help me." It wasn't until later that night that we were able to pick up Cecelia and also find out that Mike was safe.

After 9/11, I had an epiphany. I could no longer just think about myself and my wife. I had to think about my daughter and her future. It made me take a long look at myself and the things that I do. My daughter will be looking up to me as the kind of man she would one day marry. If I was a knucklehead, then I should not be surprised if Cecelia brought home a knuck-lehead boyfriend. I had to get my life in better order. Plus, I had to get back to God. I knew the Lord, but He often took a back seat to what I wanted to do. I was going about my life with little regard for God's will and purpose for me and my family. I was the very definition of a "back-sliding Christian." Yolanda was closer to God than I was, but neither of us were regular attendees at a local church. I didn't want Cecelia to grow up not knowing the Lord. Hence, Yolanda and I began our search for a church. We visited local churches, and, after many misses, we finally hit upon a church that fed us spiritually. We started attending services regularly.

The Calm Before the Storm: 6-15 years of marriage–(2002-2012)

SCOTT

I used to hear people say that having a baby changed every-thing. I didn't buy it. I would roll my eyes and dismiss it as crazy talk. But after Cecelia was born, I was a believer. No longer could

Yolanda and I just get up and go out. We had to find a babysitter. Our careers were finally taking off, too, so we had less and less time for little things. Our daily lifecycle became childcare drop off, work, home, childcare pick-up, eat, baby bedtime, and finally us time. But "we time" was reduced to us lying in bed, talking about our day, and passing out—exhausted. Boy was I ever wrong to roll my eyes at that "baby changed everything" phrase. Little did I know there were even more challenges on the horizon.

Our careers were challenging, and our responsibilities were increasing. We finally fell into a comfortable rhythm with work and Cecelia. As soon as we settled into our rhythm, we got pregnant again. We were excited but, for some reason, hesitated to share the news. We both knew that every pregnancy was unique, but Yolanda felt differently about this one. Something wasn't quite right, and we found out why. Sometime around the seventh week, Yolanda miscarried. With the exception of losing my mother, this was the hardest situation I had ever faced.

We were just getting ready to be parents again and now this new baby was taken from us. I felt a piece of me was ripped from my body without pain killers. We were nervous and excited to continue to grow our family only to have those plans abruptly halted. It was unfair. Why was this child's life ended before it had a chance to develop? We didn't even know the gender because the fetus hadn't developed that far. Although she did nothing wrong, Yolanda couldn't help but blame herself for the miscarriage. I told her that it was not her fault, and I did not, under any circumstance, blame her for it. We both were devastated. The love of God, each other, and Cecelia helped us get through our family tragedy.

To this day, I sometimes think about the child we lost and wonder whether it was a boy or a girl and who the baby would have looked like. I am not ashamed to say it took me several months to come to grips with the miscarriage. And, it's not like I really "got over" it. I just worked to channel that energy into other endeavors. I threw myself into being a better husband, father, and Christian. I rededicated myself to spending quality time with Yolanda. Auntie would come down to visit and watch Cecelia so Yolanda and I could go on date nights. I became a doting father to Cecelia and provided intentional, loving care. We would have little daddy-daughter moments where I sat down and played with her. I learned to appreciate my time with Yolanda and Cecelia because I knew tomorrow was not promised.

Rather than just sitting in the pews, I also became more active in our church. I attended Men's Ministry events, fellowshipping with godly men who poured into me spiritually. These guys helped me understand that there will be times when life doesn't work out the way you would like. Trouble will come. They shared Jesus' words found in John 16:33, "I have told you these things, so that in me you may have peace. In this world you will have trouble. But take heart! I have overcome the world." Jesus' words and the advice of the guys brought me comfort. Despite all we had experienced, Yolanda and I were starting to get better. Time became our healer—healing us through our mourning. We decided to try for another child.

When Cecelia was five years old, we welcomed Alexis to the family. Alexis was special. Her addition to our family was the salve that helped heal the wounds from the miscarriage. At birth, Alexis looked almost identical to Cecelia as a newborn. Yolanda said we had the same daughter twice. Having another child in the house changed the family dynamic again. Cecelia became our "little helper" with Alexis. She loved her new role. She would throw away diapers, clean up after herself and her little sister, and get the pacifier when Alexis needed it. Occasionally, she showed signs of jealousy over the amount of time we had to spend with Alexis. But that was to be expected. Cecelia was no longer the only child nor the baby of the family.

As time passed, with two daughters and our careers in full swing, Yolanda and I turned our attention to the church. The church we were attending had what we felt was an inadequate children's ministry. They sat the kids down in groups and taught them using Christian-themed coloring books and songs like *This is the Day That the Lord Has Made* and *This Little Light of Mine*. However, they were not getting a "children's sermon." Instead of complaining, we decided to switch churches.

We joined another mega-church with a dedicated youth ministry. We were so impressed by the organization and offerings of the ministry that we volunteered to work in it. Personally, I experienced so much spiritual growth while serving there. Doing the work of The Lord was fulfilling. I grew in my faith and learned more about the work of ministry. My personal relationship with Jesus was strengthened so much I decided to get baptized by the youth minister. It was a bold declaration of my faith. While boosting my spirituality, it also put a target on my back. I didn't realize just how big that target was until we entered into year 13 of our marriage.

YOLANDA

Have you ever seen those days when the sky was really sunny and beautiful? Then, just like that, dark clouds roll in and you are left racing for shelter as the sky opens up and the rain showers fall. No warning, no umbrella, and no change of clothes. I hate soggy socks and shoes, but towards the middle of our relationship, I felt the effects of a storm in our marriage. My shoes were soggy, and I could not explain how they got that way. It was a test...God's test. If we were going to make it, we would have to rely on him.

After forgiving my father, I grew so much spiritually. Scott and I were attending church and Bible study regularly. We were growing closer to God and each other. God was surrounding us with people who were serving Him and excelling in their lives. We vowed to stay in that lane. I finished one of my certificates and was blessed with a new job and a sizable raise. The only drawback was having to commute to Northern Virginia. It was a great opportunity but came with challenges. I would have to rearrange my schedule to make sure I could pick up Cece on time. I wanted to be home for dinner at a reasonable time every night. I realized there were things from my childhood that I wanted to be different in my home. Dinnertime was one of them. My mother had worked at night, so we seldom sat down to eat together as a family.

Life was pretty good for a while. We were enjoying being parents and our careers were blossoming. Then 9/11 hit. It was sobering for Scott and me. We had friends and family in New York City at the time and I worked not far from the Pentagon. I lost a co-worker in the attacks. Every morning I had to drive by the building with a huge gaping hole in its side as a reminder of the tragedy that had befallen our nation. Trying to process this was exhausting. I started to value my life and time, seeing it very differently. What happens if you leave the house and never return? What is the last thing I want my spouse and child to remember me saying to them? What kind of legacy do I want to leave my family? Weighty questions circulated in my head—ones yearning for answers.

Scott and I got pregnant again in 2002. Admittedly, I was under a lot of stress at work and really had not fully gotten over the chaos going on in the world. I didn't realize it at the time, but people were still in shock, and I sensed a war coming. The hole in the Pentagon was covered with plastic, not fully repaired. In a way it seemed much like our nation. This was a time to celebrate and rejoice. Seven weeks into the pregnancy, I lost the baby. I was a mess. There were so many emotions rolling around inside of me and my body reacted to each of them.

Grief is tricky. Just when you think the grief process has ended, here comes another wave. I now realize, I was not fully equipped to handle this well of grief at that time. I tried to bury myself in my work, but my body rebelled. I started having

71

phantom chest pains. My commute to work annoyed me. I felt trapped, overwhelmed. I went to see my physician. She ran a full battery of tests and determined it was stress. She warned that I had better figure it out quickly before the long-term effects started wreaking havoc on my body. I decided it was time to quit my job and find work closer to home. I was spending 2-3 hours a day in the car, depending on traffic, and coming home to my second job—being a mom. Even though I was working out, I was not resting well. I was tired all the time.

I prayed for direction. God answered and gave me the exact date to quit my job in Northern Virginia. Scott and I decided that we would take a trip to Disney World earlier than usual that year—just the two of us. We paid off everything before I resigned. I quit my job one week and the next week went to Disney World. I felt like one of those cheesy Super Bowl ads! "Hey Yolanda! You just quit your job. What are you going to do now?" Scott and I had the best time. I could finally decompress and relax. Fun and laughter truly are great medicine. I started to feel more like myself than I had in over a year.

I hadn't found a job yet, so when we returned from Florida, I finished a technical certification I was working on before looking for a new position. My stress level was more normal, and I wanted to keep it that way. We were good financially, too, which made it possible to delay finding employment.

I was also a saver. I established a "runaway account." Soon after, though, I changed its name to my "fun money/travel account" because Scott hated the term, "runaway". Apparently, it made him feel like I was judging his character. He assured me that he would not give me a reason to run away. As a result, I changed the account name. Nevertheless, Scott came to admire my wisdom with money and started a "fun money" account of his own. These accounts would come in handy during unexpected situations when we needed a break or something actually broke!

I was grateful for quality time with my family, especially with Cece. A bunch of home projects I had abandoned due to fatigue also got done. I can't tell you how many times God paid bills for us. My credit card bills would have credits, no money due, or God surprised us with extra money in our bank account. But, as they say, all good things come to an end. After my little 3-month sabbatical, I went back to work, refreshed. My commute was now only 30 minutes and I felt like I had a new life. The change made me realize the importance of valuing time over money. We all can make more money, but time is a non-renewable resource many of us do not value until it is too late.

Wrapping my mind around getting pregnant again was difficult. I was scared. If it were not for my faith and that of my husband, I am not sure I would have made the effort. We waited a whole year after the miscarriage before trying to conceive again. It gave me time to heal mentally and physically. It also gave Scott and me time to prepare. In October of 2005, our daughter Alexis was born. She was beautiful and a wonderful gift from God, especially after the miscarriage. She was a momma's girl, which was fine with me.

Scott and I had only wanted two children. So, when Alexis came, we felt that our family was complete. Scott was a great father and husband. We were not perfect, but God was definitely growing us through our trials and tests.

When Alexis was a toddler, we felt God calling us to leave Jericho to serve in Youth Ministry at Evangel Cathedral. One of our co-workers was serving there and thought we would be a great addition. This was a big step for Scott and me. We had never served in this capacity before. However, it seemed to be a great opportunity. Both of us loved kids and wanted to be of service wherever the Lord sent us.

Power Plant, as the Youth Ministry was called, was a great place for Scott and me to discover and grow our gifts and talents. Since both of us were techies, we were able to assist with technology purchases for the ministry. Scott served on the Audio/ Visual (A/V) team. Hugging and hospitality were high on my list. So, I served as "Miss Hospitality," greeting students and making them feel welcome. Right by my side were my little helpers Cece and Lexi (as they are affectionately called). Additionally, Scott and I took classes in their Bible School. The instructor led an in-depth study and we experienced God's Word in new and different ways. We were serving, learning and connecting to the kids. We felt we were really making a difference. It had such an impact on us that Scott decided to rededicate his life to Christ and get baptized a second time.

Scott's baptism was a hinge point in our lives. He was on fire for God! Our relationship got better the closer he got to Christ and living according to His Word. He was flourishing. He had passion and purpose. I could see God using him with our kids and those in Power Plant, mentoring and teaching them. Scott was growing in prayer, too. He was learning his identity in God and his role in our marriage. During this time, there was a shift in the way we related spiritually. Previously, I felt that the burden of keeping our family kingdom-focused was on me. Slowly Scott was evolving, growing, and sharing my spiritual vision for our family. We were finally committed to walking in the same spiritual direction.

Yet, in every life some rain must fall. Less than a year after Scott was baptized, we were devastated by rumors that the Power Plant Ministry may be shut down. I cried out to God, "Why did you bring us here if you were going to do this?" Then God showed me the impact the ministry had had on the teens, young adults, our children, and friends. I was humbled, but admittedly also sad. We tried to stay in the main church afterwards, but it just didn't feel right.

We left and went back to Jericho where Scott continued to serve on the Camera Ministry. Lexi and Cece were still young so I decided it would be better for us to find peace on a pew. I did not want to leave them and come back and find them running all over church since we were no longer in Youth Ministry. It was weird being back "on the bench." I had gotten used to being involved in the weekly programming of ministry and seeing all the behind-the-scenes activities. But I decided to enjoy this time and wait for God to show me where He wanted me to serve next.

Who is this person and what did you do with my *real* husband? Up until this point in our marriage, Scott and I had always had a very open and vulnerable relationship. We talked all the time. Our general sentiment about communication was that we would put it all out on the table even if it hurt. Our agreement was to be honest and deal with issues head on. In the past we welcomed difficult conversations. They were necessary if the relationship was going to work. But a change hit us hard during year 13 of our marriage.

I wish I could tell you what happened or how it started, but honestly, I can't remember. It was a slow spiral down into what I can only call a major disconnect between us. Scott had always been so loving and attentive. He was my safe place and confidante. Without warning, the temperature changed, and he suddenly became super sensitive and cold. Our rules of engagement no longer worked. I was flying blind and there was no soft-landing place.

SCOTT

All my life, I was taught a man was supposed to be a fixer. If there was a loose board on a fence, fix it. If a doorknob was wobbly, fix it. Have a problem with the Wi-Fi? Fix it. But what if the problem is you? Somewhere in the course of year 13 of my marriage, I lost focus. It was gradual and I didn't see it coming. But came it did. I was thrown way out of character. At the time, I couldn't explain what was happening. Out of what felt like nowhere, I started snapping at Yolanda for no reason. My attitude toward her soured. Little things that I used to love about her became annoyances. The cute smile she wore when explaining things looked arrogant. Her innocent inquiries about my day became irritating. She asked what was wrong, but since I didn't detect any change in my life, I told her nothing. Meanwhile, I continued to be mean to her. Any attempt to talk it out and get to the heart of the problem was met with miscommunication and frustration.

After several months of this behavior, Yolanda's patience started to wane. She was getting upset with me, and for good reason. She stopped asking me what was wrong. Instead, she ignored me. Her focus became her and the girls.

Finally, it occurred to me something was broken and needed fixing. At first, I thought it was Yolanda. (Yes, I was that far gone.) I told her those annoying little things she had been doing that worked my nerves. As you might have imagined, she didn't receive those jabs pleasantly. She had every right to be upset with me because, from her perspective, I had gone off the deep end and was acting foolishly. I couldn't figure out what was going on with me; with us. All my attempts to reach out to Yolanda to fix our relationship were met with resistance and arguments.

I was so certain she was the problem that I went to my Aunt Evelyn for advice. I had a revelation during our conversation. I was the problem! When I explained all the things Yolanda was doing, Auntie helped me to realize that Yolanda was only responding to what I was doing to her. Speaking to Auntie made me recall that famous phrase from Shakespeare's play, *Julius Caesar*, "The fault, dear Brutus, is not in our stars/But in ourselves" (*Julius Caesar*, Act I, Scene III, L. 140-141). Oh, come on! I am the cause?

It was a moment of clarity. Afterwards, God spoke to me through a song by Kirk Franklin featuring Toby Mac entitled *I am God*. The phrase, "Can I get up now?" resounded in my head. I realized I was on the ground fighting myself, my wife, and ultimately God. All this was rooted in fear. I feared I would mess up and lose Yolanda. It was that old wound resurfacing again. Even though it made no sense to be fearful of losing her, it was real in my mind. My old insecurity opened the door to fear. I took up residence in that dark and lonely place and it caused me to blow up on the love of my life.

YOLANDA

Longevity in marriage comes through evolution—no one stays the same throughout their marriage. Maintaining a connection and a common purpose is the cornerstone to enduring your partner's periods of transformation. There were certain truths about Scott and my marriage that I held on to in the middle of the storm. I knew he only wanted to be married once and loved his kids. We had a vision for our family legacy that did not include divorce. D------ was the one word we decided never to say in our home. No matter what he said or how angry he made me, I would not leave our marital bed, either. As long as he never put his hands on me, I would stay and love him, for better or for worse. Isn't that what I vowed on my wedding day? I had no idea just how hard that would be. Have mercy!

When I look back on Year 13 and 14 of our marriage, I realize they could have destroyed us if it were not for my faith and my good girlfriends, Jonetta and Caryn. I urge every married woman to find a couple of secure married women you can trust and confide in. Jonetta and Caryn encouraged me when I was really low and feeling like I didn't want to be married anymore. They reminded me of how the enemy will use a disagreement, offense, or hurt to keep us separated and, ultimately, destroy my family. Praying to God, seeking wise counsel and reading books like the *Power of the Praying Wife* by Stormie Omartian all helped me see my marriage as a place of growth during those two years.

Okay, you are probably saying, "Yolanda, that sounds great but all of us are not that mature." Honestly, neither was I. There were days when Scott made me so mad, I wanted to throw all his stuff on the porch. Even though I never left the marital bed, I would sleep on the very edge. The binding of the mattress made an imprint in my back. One rollover and I would have fallen to the floor. Oh, and while the world saw me as this strong superwoman, I was a mess. The confident woman with answers for everything at work, could not seem to figure out how to fix her marriage and get it back on track. The tears just below the surface, flowed when no one was looking. There were moments when I thought, "God why did you make me love this man so much and then do this to me? This hurts so bad. Please help me."

One day I was sitting at work. (This was the turning point for much of the strife and anger.) God broke through my pride and brought me to a place of humility. I had tried everything except surrendering to him. Scott had said something to me over a chat and I started to get emotional, so I went downstairs to my car and cried. I told God I was tired. I admitted I just couldn't do this anymore. He spoke to my spirit, "If this were your child, how would you respond?" I said, "Scott is not my child. He is a grown man and my husband. And God said, "But doesn't he deserve unconditional love, too?" I replied, "I don't even know what that looks like. I have only experienced love with conditions. If I am good or do what someone says, I receive their approval, if not, there are consequences. God answered, "Except for me. I love you unconditionally." I asked him to show me how to love unconditionally. "Help me, Lord, with my husband."

As the tears rolled down my face, I sent Scott a text message. I was tired of fighting and hurting. I also promised God I would not go home and engage with him at all. I would check on the kids and take a long hot bath, which is exactly what I did. Scott and I honestly didn't have much to say to one another. I had hoped the message about trying to love him unconditionally would serve as a white flag and we could move forward. Well, I got my answer when he walked into the bathroom. I was soaking in the tub with my candles lit to calm me. Scott came over to the tub and offered me a glass of wine. He scanned my demeanor and told me he was tired of fighting, too. We needed to find a way back to one another. I confessed that it would not be easy. I had to learn to love him unconditionally and trust him again. Also, there were some issues he needed to face head on if we were going to be together. Scott agreed, but we were not out of the woods yet. Saying you want to change and doing it is a whole other thing. We not only had communication issues, but we had to contend with family issues, as well. We had to set realistic boundaries and stick to them.

SCOTT

This was a serious demonic attack. Fully aware and with my eyes wide open I had to repair my relationship with Yolanda. I had hurt her so badly. She was well within her rights to be mad at me. I knew it would be hard for her to believe that I was really sorry for my behavior just by saying it. Earning back her trust would be an uphill climb. I knew she loved me but I also knew, at that time, she didn't like me very much. I had to humble myself, pour out my heart, and communicate with her, *really* communicate with her. I explained that I was wrestling with my identity and purpose. I had been questioning my need for a stronger connection to Christ. Fear took control and I surrendered to it, causing me to act irrationally. I used to think spiritual warfare was reserved for "super" Christians not regular people like me. I know better now.

It took me a little over a year to earn Yolanda's trust again. I inflicted deep wounds. She did not want to be vulnerable and open her heart to me. I prayed for God to stop me if I ever reverted to letting fear rule me. I never, ever wanted to put Yolanda through anything that painful for the rest of our days. No amount of pride or vanity was worth that price.

79

YOLANDA

I wish I could have waved a magic wand and, like time lapses in a movie, we could skip to our "happily ever after". That wasn't our story. It took over a year for us to rediscover who we were and what we meant to each other. Growth and progress never occur in a straight line. Sometimes we get it right and at other times miss the mark. The road to re-discovery includes some pain. We hurt each other in the process. But I looked for the lesson, applied it, and learned to forgive. I don't say "forgive and forget" because then you don't learn from the situation. When you don't understand what God is trying to teach you, you are bound to do the same thing again. We were learning not to be offensive and to forgive for the greater good of our marriage and family.

Scott and I watched a movie called *Fireproof* directed by Alex Kendrick. It was about a marriage on the verge of dissolving. The long and short of it was a lesson on making your marriage strong enough to withstand the test of time and loving one another enough to fight for it. I am not sure when Scott started doing little things for me. One day, though, I began to take notice. It felt like we were dating again. At some point I realized he was doing the Love Dare from the movie. It worked. Those unexpected little acts of love and kindness softened my heart. Our marriage slowly recovered. For our 15th anniversary we decided to renew our vows. We had made it through one of the worst storms in our lives. You could say our marriage was indeed fireproof.

At the end of the day, Scott said everything we went through was rooted in fear. Fear of not being enough. Fear of not completing his plans; fear of not being the man he wanted to be. Much later, after the rain and smoke cleared, I realized the enemy had attacked his identity after Scott rededicated his life to God.

Scott and I are stronger together. It was never about who we were individually but, who were becoming, a kingdom couple. We would have testimonies to share about how God used our marriage to grow our faith and strengthen our bond. We have a legacy of faith, love, and perseverance to leave our children, grandchildren, and their children. We had already broken so many strongholds and crippling chains in our families. Chains of unbelief, divorce, brokenness, substance abuse, mental illness and fractured relationships. I am grateful we stayed in the fight. To be honest, it was difficult. We were bruised, battered and scarred. Now on the other side, we have the victory God promises those who take the journey with Him and are obedient to His Word and will.

SCOTT

Around this time a movie premiered entitled, *Fireproof*. It was about a selfish fire captain who fought with his wife to the point of them agreeing to divorce. However, his best friend, also a firefighter, and his father convinced him to hold off on filing for divorce. They suggested a Love Dare instead, which was a 40-day marriage improvement challenge. During the dare, one spouse worked to change the way they treated their partner. The movie chronicled the captain's Love Dare experience. Ultimately, the challenge led to him and his wife reconciling.

I was inspired. Seeing the success of the Love Dare in the movie, I decided I would try it. Let me tell you, it really worked. It was a painful process. I had to alter how I treated Yolanda and, what was even more painful, practice patience as she reluctantly responded to my changed behavior. In the end, it actually worked to strengthen our bond. The Love Dare helped us weather the storm. We had to celebrate our victory. We chose to do so on our 15th anniversary.

Renewal—Beauty for Ashes

"And provide for those who grieve in Zion— to bestow on them a crown of beauty instead of ashes, the oil of joy instead of mourning, and a garment of praise instead of a spirit of despair. They will be called oaks of righteousness, a planting of the Lord for the display of his splendor."

Isaiah 61:3 NIV

SCOTT

Relieved and happy that my marriage had been restored, I wanted to do something special to commemorate it. Yolanda and I decided to get new wedding rings and renew our vows on our 15th anniversary. I wanted to go all out to show Yolanda I meant it when I apologized. So, I went on the hunt to find the perfect ring. I spent weeks going from jewelry store to jewelry store. No ring I saw screamed "Yolanda." She loves the ocean (to my wife, a year is incomplete unless she goes to the beach and sees the ocean at least once). She also exudes a simple elegance. The ring had to represent both characteristics. Frustrated yet determined, I gave up the search for a prefabricated ring and went to a custom jewelry event. At the event, I found the elements that I felt best represented Yolanda. I bought a loose blue topaz stone and had it set into a white gold band flanked by diamonds on the sides. The shank was encrusted with micro pave diamonds. The blue topaz represented the ocean. The band was a double dose of heavenly goodness with an air of simple elegance. My search was over; I had my "Yolanda" ring.

I surprised Yolanda with the ring on Valentine's Day. After dinner, I presented it to her on bended knee. "Will you remarry me?" I asked. She was so surprised. I saw that light in her eyes again. This time, she said "YES!"

YOLANDA

On Valentine's Day of 2012, Scott got down on bended knee and proposed to me over a homecooked, candlelight dinner with our girls. It was more romantic than the first proposal. He presented me with a new ring. It was gorgeous! It had a beautiful blue topaz in a white gold and diamond setting. It had special meaning to me because I always told Scott one of the reasons I love going to the beach is because it is where I feel closest to God. So, he wanted me to be reminded of that each time I looked at my beautiful ring. Scott requested I wait to wear it, though. He wanted to present it to me again at our 15th Anniversary vow renewal in August. Great! It was one of the most thoughtful things he has ever done for me.

SCOTT

We decided to have the renewal service at my cousin Clement's church in Philadelphia. Clement had left the church we were originally married in and was the pastor of a different congregation. As usual, Clement was more than happy to fulfill our request and worked with us to make the renewal special. We decided to write our own renewal vows. Again, I dug deep into my soul and poured out a heartfelt vow for Yolanda. I also purchased heart necklaces for my daughters. The necklaces symbolized my love for them. Their hearts belonged to daddy until their husbands won them from me. The ceremony was beautiful. The entire family played a role in it. Cecelia played the violin for us and both Cecelia and Alexis came up to the altar to receive their heart necklaces.

YOLANDA

August is a major month for our family as it is filled with many birthdays and anniversaries. In particular, my birthday is the 8th and our anniversary is the 9th. When we were engaged, Scott said he liked it that way because he would never forget our

83

anniversary. I like it, too. I have a summer birthday and we can go away to celebrate *Birthdayversary*! It is a win-win! After two very challenging years filled with so much craziness, it was time to celebrate the beauty that had come from those ashes. We had left behind quite a bit of our old selves and our marriage now reflected a deeper understanding of our God and one another.

This time, as I stood at the altar, I could honestly say I was ready to submit to the new and improved version of my husband and trust in his love. It was a love now tested by time and trial. We had risen from the ashes with new knowledge and hard-earned wisdom. So now that we had survived the worst two years of our marriage, what were we going to do? Go to Disney World! We celebrated my 40th Birthday and our 15th year of marriage surrounded by our family and close friends in Disney's fun-filled, fantasy land.

16 - 22 years of marriage—(2013-2019)
In It to Win It

YOLANDA

Scott and I were finally back on the same page. Now we could concentrate on working on our dreams, aspirations, and a new vision for our marriage. There were a few goals we had set for ourselves earlier we had not yet achieved.

Cece was now in middle school and Lexi in elementary school. Both the girls were growing so fast they didn't need us to do as much for them anymore. They were beautiful, smart and very independent. After achieving multiple technical certifications, one of my managers suggested I should pursue a life coach certification. I had no idea what it entailed. However, she assured me I was already doing it so I might as well be certified.

I researched different programs and decided to attend a coaching intensive through *Valorie Burton's Coaching and Positive*

Psychology Institute. I had read several of her books. I liked her coaching style, and she was relatable. I started the Coaching Intensive in Virginia. As I neared completion, I called Scott and asked him if he would support me going for the full certification, which would take another six months. He agreed. I give him credit, he did a wonderful job helping with the kids, cooking, and cleaning so I could finish the program in February of 2014.

In 2013, we once again changed churches. Scott and I jumped into ministry with a renewed excitement. This time he would become a part of the men's ministry and I would work with the kid's ministry. I also joined a women's bible study and worked with my daughter Lexi's group, which needed a small group leader. Scott taught on Sunday mornings, and I led the small groups for youth. Eventually, I was asked to be on the bible study leadership team. The team's responsibility was to lead small, bible study groups.

A couple of years before, I led a prayer group in my home. It was called the BIG Prayer group. It was comprised of women from 5 different states and we held meetings in each other's homes. We read devotions and prayed for one another. We grew to love one another and are still in contact today. This group prepared me for the task of leading children and women in their faith walk and relationship with Christ. I did this for a few years until Scott got the infamous *post card* in the mail.

What postcard you might ask? The one that would change our lives for the next three years as Scott pursued his dream of becoming a Doctor of Science. I wanted Scott to realize his dream. We had to figure out a new family dynamic and schedule and how to navigate the kids through middle and high school. If you recall, back when we were dating, Scott was pursing a PhD. When he became frustrated, he left the program.

This was Scott's last chance to finish what he started. The difference between then and now was the school was farther away and we had jobs and kids to manage. But we had always supported one another's dreams. This was no different. Scott attended the information session twice before finally deciding to apply and start the program. No turning back; we were in it.

Lexi started middle school and Cece started her junior year of high school during the first year of Scott's doctoral program. I had no idea what an emotional roller coaster I had signed up for. "Welcome to single parenthood," I thought to myself. To support the family while Scott was in school, I opted for a 4-day work week. It was a wise decision and helped me manage my life and the kids. Yet, I still felt like I had no time for myself. Between the emotional meltdowns of two teenage girls and managing my clients at work, I was worn out. Scott was juggling school and work so, at times, we felt a little disconnected. He had his cohort of school mates with whom he shared his experiences. So at times I felt kind of alone. Due to Scott's workload, regular date nights and time alone was no longer the norm. Despite the challenges, we still coordinated our schedules to get away at least once a year for a few days to ourselves.

I stepped away from Women's Ministry at the church. I still worked with the teens, though, as I now had a child in middle school. Cece was preparing for college in the Fall. Scott was entering his final year of school. We were almost there—one more year! But life, never to be outdone, would throw me another curve ball.

Remember my sister Kisha? Well, we had not fully mended our strained relationship, but we were a least able to have civil conversations. I thought we were on our way to better days. Then, I got the first of three, life-changing phone calls.

It was a crazy summer, Cece had vacillated between wanting to go to school and staying home because she was scared. Scott had to leave for his program the week we were scheduled to move her into the dorm. Since he was not at home, I had to arrange for other people to come and help me load her up and see her off.

I was asleep when the phone rang. It was my niece who said they found my sister on the bathroom floor. I must have gasped as she continued with the preliminary assessment, they thought she was dead. Honestly, I thought I heard her incorrectly. Or was I dreaming? Did she say *dead*? I asked my niece, "Did you call the paramedics?" She told me the paramedics were already at the house working on her. My mom showed up at Kisha's place and grabbed the phone from my niece. Mom told me she would call me back. An hour later, I received a call from my dad. My sister, Kisha, was pronounced dead at the hospital. There was nothing they could do. It was after four o' clock in the morning. Yet I knew I would not be able to go back to sleep.

I lay in bed sobbing for about an hour. In my grief, something inside told me I was going to need backup. I was in shock and alone. I called Scott and he was just as devastated as I. Although he wanted to come home immediately, he had just gotten to school and needed to finish his program. So, I told him to stay. I sent out a message to my prayer group and four of my closest sorority sisters. One of them, Caryn, called me immediately and asked me how I was doing. Instinctively she asked, "Where is Scott?" When I told her Scott was at school and I was alone, she packed a bag and came to stay with me until Scott could come home. My Aunt Evelyn came in later that day with some of my other sorority sisters and friends. Their presence and support may have been the only reason I didn't break down and shut myself up in my room.

You really don't know who your friends are until trouble comes. There were people I thought would be there for me, who were not. I found comfort from unexpected places and people. It was a blessing. I learned some valuable lessons during that time about love, forgiveness, and comforting others when they are grieving. I use those lessons often.

If only that had been the end of it, but it wasn't. Did you ever hear that saying, "Death comes in threes?" Well, that was exactly what happened in my family. After losing my sister in August, I lost my uncle in December of the same year, and my cousin the following February. Amidst all this I was searching for a new job.

In January, after my uncle died, I thought I would lose my mind. I was tired of everything. I was still processing my sister's death and now one of my favorite uncles was gone. It had been a difficult adjustment with Cece being at school. I had not been prepared for the new norm in our home. People I thought were close friends seemed to just walk away leaving me broken. It really hurt. I was exhausted and way over my limit and I knew it. But how could I stop? Scott tried to talk to me, but only made it worse. We ended up screaming at each other, which resulted in a long overdue ugly cry session in my bathroom. When it was over and my tear ducts completely empty, I could breathe again.

Repositioning

YOLANDA

The year 2019 was a year of transitioning and repositioning. My cousin passed away in February and I kept wondering when God was going to give us a break. I am grateful that he didn't make me wait too long. In February, I was offered and accepted a new position that would be a relatively easy move. Scott finished his doctoral degree and Cece survived her freshman year of college. As God would have it, our time was up at our current church, so we had a break from serving in ministry, as well. God was moving us again into new places and different spaces. We had learned so much about mindsets and ministry, but it was time to go.

During the summer we celebrated my mom's 80th birthday. My sister, Betty and I said we all needed a party, but mom especially. She had lost her daughter, brother, and nephew over a 6-month period. It was so beautiful to watch my mom sing and enjoy her family and friends after such a tumultuous year. Even in her grief, my mom exuded strength, a resilient faith, and a warm and loving spirit. Her strength bolstered mine. The party was a time to celebrate mom's life and honor my sister, as well. It was a healing moment for all of us. Life is but a vapor. It would never be the same again. We needed to move on, to live.

In August we went to Disney World. It is our happy place. I love to go there. I indulge the dreamer and little girl inside, who just wants to play all day. We celebrated my birthday and our anniversary, again, grateful God had let us share another year together. Scott and I decorated a Mickey cake and had dinner that night, just the two of us. The kids were off soaking in all the fun they could before returning to the real world.

In December 2019, we paid off our home and celebrated it as our Christmas gift to one another. I enjoyed the moment, reflecting on God's grace and goodness in guiding us through it all. We had survived. We could now share an amazing testimony of our love and faith.

SCOTT

After our renewal ceremony, life took some more twists and turns. We started attending another church and made a return to Children's Ministry. Yolanda was a small group leader and discipled a group of young middle school girls, which included Alexis. I taught at "Large Group" (essentially, the "kid's sermon") for the kindergarten through second grade children. It was interesting to hear the questions the little ones asked. Many of them were more insightful and thought-provoking than those asked by adults. Even Cecelia became active and started attending the High School Ministry. In addition, both Yolanda and I got involved in Women's and Men's Ministry, respectively. The years in that church's Kids' Ministry were very fulfilling and rewarding for the whole family.

As a part of building her business, Yolanda enrolled in Valorie Burton's Coaching and Positive Psychology (CaPP) Institute. In the program, Yolanda learned advanced coaching skills, applied positive psychology concepts, and business development action plans which helped her generate coaching opportunities. I was very proud of her commitment to pursuing and building a business. It was a major step in the right direction for her. While she was completing the coursework, I took care of the girls and ran the household. I have always fully supported Yolanda's educational and business goals, this was no different. One of the great things about our marriage is the mutual support of each other's goals, even when old goals resurfaced.

In 2015, I received an unsolicited postcard in the mail inviting me to an information session about a Doctor of Science in Information Systems and Communications degree program at Robert Morris University in Pittsburgh, PA. I showed the card to Yolanda, and she asked if I requested it. I said no and threw it away. Even though one of my long-term goals was to finish a doctoral degree, I couldn't afford it and didn't really have the time to pursue it. I put it out of my mind until another postcard showed up in my mailbox. Was this a sign from God? After talking about it with Yolanda, I decided to go hear what they had to say. The session was in Washington, DC, so I drove into the city and listened to the sales pitch. As impressive as the program sounded, I left the meeting without committing to it. Once again, I felt like I neither had the money nor the time to do it.

About six months later, I received yet another postcard inviting me to the information session. I had to give it to them, they were persistent. What more could they say about this program? I decided to humor them again and show up to the meeting. The professors remembered me from the last session and jokingly told me that I had better sign up or they were going to charge me for the hors d'oeuvres and beer I consumed. I took the information home (again). I thought long and hard about the program and even prayed about it.

Was God up to something? Was this what He wanted me to do? I got my answer in the form of a benefit at my new job: tuition reimbursement. I did the math, calculating my out-of-pocket expenses. The program no longer seemed out of my price range. Furthermore, the professors informed me of available scholarship money to help with the cost. That settled it; it was a done deal.

I brought all the information to Yolanda and told her I was interested in doing it. She agreed. Yolanda understood I still wanted to be Doctor Scott Lupton, though my first venture into doctoral studies was rather painful. After much prayer, careful deliberation, and an endorsement from my wife, in the Fall of 2016, I started my journey to become the next Doctor Lupton.

The Doctor of Science in Information Systems and Communications degree program was an *executive style* program, meaning I only went to Pittsburgh for one full week at the beginning of each semester (in August and January) and one weekend a month for the remaining months. The rest of the time, we worked remotely from home. It meant I wasn't away from my family for too long at any one time. It was an intense, accelerated three-year program. I would not have time to linger on any step of the program because the next step arrived quickly. This arrangement seemed like it would fit well into my lifestyle. That is until it got in the way.

Having to be in Pittsburgh for a week in January was a challenge. The weather was unpredictable at that time of the year. Worse yet, it also meant cutting our Christmas vacation short, as I was due in Pittsburgh the first full week of January. Also, being away for a week in August meant I missed some significant milestones. My first August residency week caused me to miss Alexis' first day of middle school. I'm usually there for my girls. This time I was not. I felt like a negligent dad, but Alexis didn't make a big deal of it. She understood that daddy was in school, too, and she was proud of me.

By far, the biggest events missed while attending the August residency of my last year occurred simultaneously: Cecelia's first day of college and the passing of my sister-in-law. Both were significant events. While I was in Pittsburgh working on my studies and hanging out with my cohort, Yolanda was preparing to take Cecelia to move-in day for her freshman year in college. Since I was not there, Yolanda asked Auntie to come down from New Jersey to assist. The night before Cecelia's move-in day, Yolanda received a phone call from her parents. They told her Kisha, her older sister, had passed away suddenly. After the initial shock, Yolanda called me. I was already in bed when the phone rang. I was exhausted after an intense day of coursework and lectures. It took me several minutes to understand what Yolanda was saying. She was breathing hard, crying, and incoherent. When I finally made out what she was saying, I fired back a line of questions. What? Kisha is dead? Oh, my Lord! What happened?

Time stopped dead in its tracks. Kisha is gone? I said, "How are you doing, Yolanda? I am coming home tomorrow." She said, "No, don't. Stay at school. I will be fine." I was torn. I knew her sister's loss was hard to handle. Kisha was only 15 months older than Yolanda and a year younger than me! How could this be? Yolanda must be a mess. I knew I was a mess.

I hated dealing with death. It hurt even more when it was a loved one who passed. Even though time has healed the wound of losing my mother, I never really got used to losing any close relatives or friends. Old pangs of grief and anguish rushed over me. This was difficult. I was a mess the rest of my residency for obvious reasons. I called Yolanda at every break between classes and each evening. I was grateful for Auntie and Caryn, one of Yolanda's sorority sisters. They were there to comfort and help Yolanda in my absence. I felt like a chump for not leaving school and rushing home to be with my wife in her time of need. Yolanda would not hear of it. She insisted I finish my residency. "This is your last year. You're almost there. Don't stop now." Yolanda was so wise and selfless. God bless her.

I drove home in a blur. I don't even remember making all my exits and turns. I called Yolanda to let her know where I was and that I was on my way home. I couldn't seem to get there quick enough. When I arrived home, I went inside and held Yolanda for what seemed to be an eternity. "Baby, I am so sorry. Please forgive me for not coming home sooner." "I know," she said, "I'm just glad you're here now."

It was only by the grace of God that I graduated on time. In hindsight, I must have been crazy to even attempt it! How in the world did I manage to complete my doctorate while being a husband, father, and information technology professional? But alas, I am now Doctor Scott Lupton. We finished off the summer by going to our happy place, Walt Disney World. What a relief it was to go away in August and not be sitting in a classroom. We had the whole family with us: Yolanda, me, Cecelia, Alexis, Auntie, and our niece Maya, Kisha's daughter. It was a great family time and we were afforded the opportunity to be kids again. We were together and happy in spite of all the mess we had been through. We capped off the year by paying off our house. Hallelujah!

TIME OUT
What foundational issues shaped our marriage experience?

YOLANDA

Forgiveness can strengthen your bond with your spouse; unforgiveness destroys trust which, ultimately, does eternal damage to the relationship. Forgiveness is a demonstration of love and commitment. Unforgiveness unravels the threads which hold the relationship together.

Unconditional/Committed love can only be accomplished when both parties are equally committed to the relationship and to God. Each must view the relationship above their individual feelings and goals. It is a love that never says never and does not quit, no matter the trial.

Shared Goals and Vision are the aims of a committed love. The marriage flows and grows because you are working together *for* something good. Your marriage should have purpose. Each partner is accountable to the other to ensure they are moving in the same direction, simultaneously. Whatever you envision for your marriage, regularly revisit the goals you have set and stop to celebrate the achievements and the milestones reached.

SCOTT

Spiritual Growth brings inner peace and fortifies you when you or your relationship are under attack. Studying God's Word and serving the Lord are exercises for the spirit, mind, and soul. It provides discernment and spiritual insight which are needed if your relationship is going to thrive and not just survive.

Self-Reflection is important. You are responsible for you. When you are feeling out of sorts, stop and take inventory. You cannot expect your spouse to understand what you are feeling, if you are not in tune with your own thoughts, feelings and inner rhythm. Until your spouse understands what is going on with you, they will be a reflection of the turmoil you feel.

Lesson Sharing

Lesson One: Reflect—Marriage is *Real* Work—Marriage is not for the faint of heart. It is work, *real* work. Sometimes you will have to fight, long and hard for it. Every challenge, every setback, every trial, and every accomplishment is a stepping stone to something bigger and better. You will have to grow through the muck and mire to get there. But it will be worth it.

1. What were some ideals or expectations you had when you were first married? How did those change over time?
2. What are some of the ways you and your spouse are intentional about making time for one another?
3. For Scott and me, the events of 9/11 were a milestone moment in our lives and marriage. What are some of these moments in your marriage? How did they affect your relationship with your spouse? For example, did you to see them from two different perspectives? Did it affect the way you communicated with your spouse? Write those moments down. Share and discuss them together.

Lesson Two: Relate—Sacrifice leads to Growth in Marriage— For better or for worse means just that. We all like the "for better" part, but we don't always want to accept the "for worse" part. Yet, we promise both at the altar. Growth happens in the "for worse" part where the growth happens. We discover who we are when our backs are against the wall.

1. Are you willing to sacrifice for your partner?
2. Are you only in the relationship solely for the benefits, what you can get from it?
3. What challenges and trials have you faced with your spouse and how did you overcome them?
4. During times of frustration and stress, how do you communicate with your spouse?
   a. Are you calm under pressure?
   b. What things have you learned about your spouse in times of trial or uncertainty?
   c. How can you support and comfort your spouse during these times?

5. Does your marriage have a mission statement?
    a. Have you and your spouse talked openly about your dreams and set a vision for your family?
    b. Have you established goals you want to achieve together? Now would be a great time to do so! Take a weekend trip and dream together. Talk about goals you want to achieve as individuals and as a couple. Develop a plan, a timeline, and a checklist. Check them off, one by one.

Lesson Three: Reveal—A Good Marriage Honors God— Marriage is about glorifying God and not us. Surely, we benefit, but God gets the glory when we sacrifice for one another. We honor God when we love one another unconditionally. The grace God grants to us and we want from others, is the same grace we need to give. Also, we need to forgive as God has forgiven us. It is a lot harder than it sounds, but we are living proof it is possible.

1. What is your definition of unconditional love?
    a. How does that line up with what God says about love in I Corinthians, Chapter 13?
    b. How do you display this to your spouse?
2. *"Therefore, as God's chosen people, holy and dearly loved, clothe yourselves with compassion, kindness, humility, gentleness and patience. Bear with each other and forgive one another if any of you has a grievance against someone. Forgive as the Lord forgave you. And over all these virtues put on love, which binds them all together in perfect unity."* (Colossians 3:12-13 NIV) Discuss this passage of Scripture with your spouse. This is one of those verses that calls us to examine our character and challenges us to take action in our relationships.
    a. Are you holding on to unforgiveness towards anyone in your life right now? If so, write it down and pray about how God would have you to resolve it.

b. Are you are holding onto unforgiveness with your spouse? Make time to discuss the issue and how to deal with it moving forward. We do not want to block our own blessings because we can't forgive others.

3. Grace is defined as the love of God shown to the unlovely; the peace of God given to the restless; and the unmerited favor of God. (https://www.christianity.com/theology/what-is-grace.html) We don't need grace when we are at our best. Conversely, we need it when we have fallen short; when we are far from our best.

a. In what ways have you seen grace exhibited in your marriage?

b. Who tends to extend grace more often, you or your spouse? Scott and I have this little reminder of ways we show grace to one another.

   G—Giving unconditional love
   R—Releasing blame and granting forgiveness
   A—Acting in kindness and humility
   C—Comforting one another
   E—Exercising our faith by praying for our spouse
   Develop your own acronym or affirmation as a reminder to extend grace to your spouse.

Final Thoughts on the 'MARRIAGE: BECOMING ONE...' Chapter

Scott and I have said from the very beginning of our marriage, if we stick together, it is us against the world. We are Team Lupton, as we like to call ourselves. We were challenged but remain a team even as we were overcome by the waves of fear and miscommunication. When we are being pulled into the ocean's undertow, the only way to get back to shore is to swim against it. If you have ever tried to do this, you know how difficult it can be. The sand beneath your feet pulls in the opposite direction of where you want to go. This is what marriage feels like when your spouse is drifting away. You can see them but are helpless to prevent it. We are no longer standing back-to-back as a tower of strength against the world, but face-to-face at a distance from one another. We become unwilling to bridge the divide because we see the other person as our enemy.

Call for help. If we don't, we will surely be swept out to sea. Luckily, there are lifeguards at the beach to save you if you miscalculate and end up in danger. We also have a God who guards our lives and watches over our marriages. We just have to remember to ask for help. Sometimes he sends it in the form of friends who speak life into your situation or your heart. Other times, he sends a song, class, or counselor that can pierce through our pride and speak to our pain.

Humility and forgiveness are key to relational vulnerability. This can be a challenge in a "Me-first" culture, but the Kingdom of God is upside down. Jesus said, to truly love, we must first serve. The best place to practice this is in our own homes with our spouses and children. When you want to lash out remember that you and your spouse are intricately intertwined. Your children are watching how you work together through challenges as well as successes. What legacy of love are you leaving to them by the way you behave in your home?

Cecelia 2020

Alexis 2021

BLINDSIDED
Marriage In A Pandemic

What in the world is going on?

SCOTT

Let me be transparent, 2020 was a crazy year. As we were getting ready for our summer plans, the world went haywire. Not long after Yolanda and Auntie returned from their girl's trip and Cece came home for spring break, news broke about a virus spreading rapidly worldwide. At first I was skeptical, thinking it was just another flu. It was nothing to panic about. Plus, it had not yet made it to the United States. However, I soon realized just how much I underestimated COVID-19.

When I heard a man in the United States had died from COVID-19 in February, I still maintained it was not that serious. Of course, we were still living our lives as though nothing was wrong. Yolanda and Aunt Evelyn (Auntie) went to the 2-day *If: Gathering* in Texas, and Cece was winding down from school, preparing for spring break. My thoughts were that this would pass, and we would be fine. It didn't get serious until Cece was told not to return to school after spring break in March.

At that time, Yolanda and I were still going in to work and Lexi was still going to school. Only Cece was affected. However, that changed rapidly. Lexi was told to stay home and begin distance learning much like her sister. The president declared a national emergency on March 13 and the country pretty much shut down soon thereafter. Things got serious when they finally told Yolanda and me to stay home and do not come to work.

That stay-at-home mandate came with little details about whether we would be paid. This uncertainty was very stressful. What did this mean? Just because we were forced to stay at home didn't mean we would not have bills to pay. And what if one of us contracted COVID-19? Would my insurance still cover us even though I was not physically working? How could I be certain my family and I would be cared for given this mandate? This really tested my faith. I worked to keep a happy face in front of my daughters but secretly I was worried.

As God would have it, both Yolanda and I were considered *essential workers* and our respective companies were able to pay us via the Paycheck Protection Program or some other established measure. Also, the company I worked for kept me abreast of the details of the shutdown from the company's perspective. We were told to stay home, and that they were working on supporting us. That provided some comfort because through it I was able to pay our bills and cover us in case of medical emergencies. God is so good.

Life during the shutdown

SCOTT

Having to stay home full time was the next challenge. Thank God we all were together. We didn't have to worry about the whereabouts of our girls. Yolanda and I were already "clean freaks" so we already had sufficient cleaning supplies on hand. Things we used to do as part of our regular household shopping paid off. When we went shopping, we would routinely purchase cleaning supplies to have as backup. We found stashes of Clorox wipes and Lysol throughout the house. In fact, I had just bought a mega pack of wipes right before the pandemic started. But now that the shutdown was in full swing, we had to think about the long game. How long would we be forced to stay at home? How could we replenish supplies as we used them? Would we be able to get enough food? Would we be able to stay safe?

All these questions forced Yolanda and me to become creative in running the household. Super sleuth Yolanda joined a Facebook group of people who were on the hunt for cleaning supplies. Through that group, she found out which local stores had supplies in stock. We went to those stores and waited in long lines. I got up early to go to a Target that was rumored to have wipes. I was third in line when the store opened, I went straight to the cleaning supply aisle and found some. Success! I was officially "about that life" and dedicated my energy and time searching for cleaning supplies. Later Yolanda switched gears searching online. I was shocked at the number of online stores she found with inventory. Boxes of cleaning products started arriving at the house soon thereafter. We had a system, and that system was working. Amen for that.

We had similar success in food shopping. At first, I would venture out to the local supermarkets to buy food. The stores would be crowded and many of the food items had low or no stock. But as the pandemic got worse, COVID cases started to rise and food shopping became more challenging. I didn't feel safe walking through the grocery stores even with my mask on. We used a meal kit service that sent boxes to our house. It was great. To supplement, we found a few local restaurants who sold meat and vegetables. Since they could not safely open, they delivered them. Between that and Instacart service, we regularly had food delivered to us. Thank God for those brave delivery men and women. They helped us immensely.

With cleaning supplies and food covered, all we had to do was peacefully co-exist with one another. It had been a while since we all lived together as a family. Cece had been away at college, and we were used to having only one daughter at home. Since we were all together, adjustments had to be made. We ate more food and used more supplies. I can say we actually enjoyed our family time.

I was home now and couldn't really go anywhere. This gave me the opportunity to complete some home improvement projects I had been putting off. I found doing these projects were a much-appreciated distraction. Instead of thinking about the pandemic and the unknown, I got my hands dirty and engaged my mind in constructive things. One such project was restoring our deck. Cece and I stained the deck, painted the fence around it, and painted the planters on each end of it. Afterwards, Yolanda put her touch on it and bought some new chairs, a bench, end tables and an outside area rug. The deck became our "staycation" oasis. We spent several days researching our project plan and working on the deck, and evenings relaxing and enjoying it, especially the firepit. Funny, we had never really spent any significant time on the deck in previous years. However, this year we maximized our deck time.

The longer I stayed home the more I started to realize what was truly important in my life. God was taking care of my bills and salary, so I had time to focus. I was happier and less stressed when I spent quality time with Yolanda and my daughters. I found solace in being safe at home with them. I worked on my relationship with God, improving myself, and my bond with Yolanda and my girls. Those things were more important to than any title at work or large paycheck. Money can come and go, but time is a non-renewable asset. Once it is gone, you cannot recover it. I made better use of my time spending it with

God, Yolanda, and my daughters than striving for a bigger pay-check or a fancier title.

Yolanda and I made time to connect with each other and get closer. We both took time to learn something new each day and spend quality time together in the evenings. This book, for instance, was written during this period. We also started having date nights. We would go to our room to watch a movie and eat dinner together. The girls didn't mind because they had run of the living room television and could watch whatever they wanted. I had to admit, I rather enjoyed reconnecting with Yolanda. Funny how much more attention I gave her when I had no work distractions to divert my thoughts. We would talk about how we both had some trepidation about the pandemic. We prayed for not only our safety, but that of our parents and extended family.

I hated not being able to solve this crisis on my own. I felt like it was my job, as the man of the house, to solve problems that affected the safety of my wife and daughters. But there was nothing I could do about this one. Yolanda reminded me that God was in charge, and I had to trust Him. This pandemic forced me to cast all my hopes and fears on Him and trust that He would take care of them all.

> *Blessed are those whose help is the God of Jacob, whose hope is in the Lord their God. He is the Maker of heaven and earth, the sea, and everything in them—he remains faithful forever.*

> Psalms 146:5-6 NIV

Yolanda explained how much she had to deal with while I was in Pittsburgh working on my doctorate. I also heard her heart. She explained I seemed distant at times. As painful as that was to hear, I took it in and thought about how she must have felt and what she experienced. I did a brain pause, switching to her perspective. It helped shed light on some of my habits which were difficult for my wife to handle. Regrettably, I put other tasks and accomplishments ahead of her. Also, by not telling her know what I was thinking or how I was feeling, I was shutting her out of my life. That was a tough pill to swallow.

I realized I had to rededicate myself to being more communicative and intentional with my wife. I thought I was good at communicating, but I realized I needed more work in that area. One of Yolanda's love languages is quality time. Spending quality time with her gave me valuable insights into how to communicate my love to her. As we navigated the pandemic, we wondered if other married couples had similar issues and concerns. To that end, Yolanda and I decided to listen to God and get involved in the married couple ministry at our church.

Both of us had served in various capacities at churches in the past, but we never served together as a team. Starting a marriage eGroup (a term used at Elevation Church for online bible study groups) was a first for us. We hoped that by leading the group, we would have a way to chat with other married couples and gain valuable insights and lessons from their marriages that could help ours. The eGroup, which Yolanda cleverly named *REALationship Matters* since we were going to discuss real relationship matters, turned out better than we anticipated. Our blessing was having other couples to talk to during this season. They poured into us. The group consisted of couples ranging from less than one year to over 30 years of marriage. They had a wealth of experience and knowledge and were willing to share with all of us. And to think, at first, I was reluctant to start the eGroup. I was worried we wouldn't have couples who consistently showed up to the meetings. Once again, God proved me wrong and reinforced my trust in Him.

Yolanda got called back to work just as we were making strides in restoring our family rhythm, communication, and connection. Since she was considered an essential employee, her employer, the US Government, requested she and her co-workers return to the office. That really put a damper on our bonding time and threw Yolanda back into her stressful work environment. Two months later, I was called back, as well.

When I returned to the office, the pandemic was still active. We remained under a mask mandate and practiced social distancing. We worked on an alternating schedule where half of the team was in one week while the other half stayed home and vice versa. What I quickly realized was I didn't like what I was doing anymore. Had I really enjoyed coming into the office pre-pandemic? I had been thriving at home for so long I lost my desire to return.

The software development work I did required I come into the office. Going into the office meant dealing with the stressors of unrealistic demands and indecision. I was blessed to have a job and didn't take that lightly or for granted. But the fact remained I simply did not feel safe there and my time would be better spent working from home. When I was in the office, I dealt with ever changing requirements, perpetual code rewrites and other documentation. I was stuck in an unhealthy cycle. It was time for a change. For the next few weeks, my evenings were spent working on my exit strategy and searching for a new job. I searched for a job which allowed me the flexibility to work from home and not have to report to a government facility. I put my trust in God to provide one for me.

That fall, my stepmother Monica (dad and Monica got married a year before Yolanda and I did) called to tell me dad had congestive heart failure and had been rushed to the hospital. As if dealing with COVID wasn't enough, now I had this to add to my worries. She coordinated a Zoom family meeting to give us all the information at once. Monica convened my brother Mike, his wife Michelle, my brother Steve, Yolanda and me on the call and provided the details of Dad's condition. Monica assured us Dad was getting better and the doctors were stabilizing him. Thank

You Jesus. She also mentioned that due to COVID restrictions, she was not able to see Dad after he was admitted to the hospital.

I couldn't take losing another parent right now. I believed God was bigger than this setback. My faith got a boost because God was working this out in dad's favor (and mine). I really needed that reassurance in this season. I knew this had to be especially hard for Monica since she couldn't visit Dad in the hospital. Yolanda and I continued to pray for them both.

The rest of the year was spent dealing with the aftereffects of working during the pandemic and the routine of cleaning, sanitizing, and mask wearing. I was contacted by several companies about a position. Some even made offers. I was encouraged, but since none met my firm *work from home* requirement, I respectfully declined them.

2021, A New Year

SCOTT

Now that 2020 was behind us, we could start the new year refreshed and ready, right? If only that were true. By the time 2021 rolled in, not much had changed. We were still punch drunk from a tumultuous 2020 and COVID was still in effect. In addition, Lexi was not adjusting well to distance learning, and she began to crack under the pressure. Will this madness ever end? Never in my life have I had to deal with so many emotions. Spiritual growth, communication enhancement, intentionality, parenting, and work stresses all landed on my plate. This was enough to drive me insane. If ever I needed help, it was now. It was warfare and surely meant something big was on the horizon. Why else would I be going through so much?

God reminded me that even when things seem bleak, there is always hope in Him. In January I received what I thought was yet another random email from a company recruiter. I respectfully responded to his inquiry about my availability and asked him what positions he was proposing. His response was intriguing. He said there were several open positions, some of which offered the opportunity to work from home. That piqued my curiosity. After several back-and-forth email discussions, I landed an interview.

God orchestrated the whole thing because I had recently started working on several new tasks in my current job that mapped directly to the needs of the prospective position. I did well in the interview and the recruiter helped me with the next steps. After discussing the terms and negotiating what amounted to a 7.5% pay raise, I received an offer in early April. A benefit of the new position was the ability to work from home (and to report to a non-government office when I didn't work from home).

Before I could celebrate and send in my resignation, paperwork had to be processed. The paperwork took months to go through. April passed into May. May carried over into June. I was still in my current job, and I couldn't tell them that I had a new job because the paperwork had not gone through the process. Government bureaucracy at its finest! I began to worry, and anxiety took hold of me. Was this job really going to happen? Am I doomed, trapped in my current position? Why was this new job being dangled in my face, just out of reach? Just when I resigned to start the job hunt over again, the paperwork finally was processed.

I started the new job at the end of June. God timed it so well I didn't even have a gap in paychecks. My last paycheck from the old job came on the same day as my first paycheck of my new job. God is always on time!

The beauty of this new job was twofold. Not only did I get what I asked for in terms of the ability to work from home, but the extra money allowed Yolanda to leave her job, as well. I was able to support Yolanda's dream just as she did for me when I went back to school for my doctorate. I give God the glory.

The World Turned Upside Down

YOLANDA

Recently, Scott woke up and discovered he had a flat tire. He went to put the spare on the car, and it was flat, too. After putting air in the spare and missing his initial appointment, he drove the car to the shop for repair. While there, the mechanic discovered two of the other tires were damaged, as well. Four tires and many hours later, Scott returned home exhausted by what first seemed a simple task. All in all, it had snowballed taking a day's worth of time and energy. Oh, and this all happened on the day we were supposed to drive to New Jersey to celebrate a belated Father's Day with my dad. This was indicative of what 2020 felt like.

Mentally, 2020 was an overwhelming year filled with uncertainty and chaos. It felt as if the world had come unhinged. There were so many unknowns and it wreaked havoc in many people's relationships and marriages. Families had to redefine how they interacted and what they really knew about one another. Parents saw their kids in new ways. They were thrust into new roles. Many became more involved in educating their kids remotely, while trying to work themselves. Each day was different, with new discoveries and information, yet the same uncertainties.

Some children were stressed. New anxieties arose around health and survival they had never experienced. Suddenly, some parents were jobless, homeless, and hopeless as the pandemic caused food insecurity, housing, education inequities, and healthcare issues. Not only did we have to consider these issues for our immediate family but extended family, as well. Adult kids moved back home. Families made difficult decisions regarding the best way to care for elderly parents and relatives as suddenly long-term care facilities became hot beds of infection, illness, and death.

It was a year of self-reflection and redirection. Couples started spending more time together and discovered some interesting things about themselves, their spouses and their relationships. During this time, Scott and I discovered that we still had some issues bubbling just beneath the surface that we needed to resolve. Overall, we were still very much in love. We needed to address a lack of intentionality which had slowly crept into our relationship. We had to get back to making what mattered most a priority and not all the other things that might take us where we want to go in the long run. I am not sure how we got here? But we needed to do what was necessary to get back on track?

As we stated in the previous chapter, the loss of my sister took a serious mental toll on me, so did Scott's being in school for 3 years working on his doctorate degree. If that wasn't enough, my job became boring. Scott was finished with his degree. Now, I started wondering, "What's next for me?"

In January of 2020, we started working with our good friend who was a financial advisor. We evaluated our financial situation and made sure we were on track to achieve our long-term goals. We had no idea less than 6 months later we would be facing a pandemic that would put our financial stability and very lives at stake.

The first months of the pandemic jarred us. My eldest daughter came home from college for spring break and didn't return because campus housing was closed to stop the spread of COVID-19 in the dorms. The following Friday an edict came from my youngest daughters' high school. They decided to change to remote learning due to the pandemic. The whole world was slowing down and closing to stop the spread of the virus. Scott and I were still going to work, but we had no idea just how bad things were about to get. Like so many others, mid-April we were told to stay home and not come back to work until further notice. One of our first thoughts was are we going to get paid while we are working from home? What happens now?

Honestly, it was kind of hard to sleep over the next few weeks. There was so much uncertainty. Deaths were rising in the country and in our community of friends. A close friend lost her father to COVID. For me, this truly drove home the seriousness of our situation. Most of the mundane things we often took for granted like grocery shopping, going to the mall and hugging someone could potentially bring the virus home to our loved ones. At first, we didn't fully understand how it spread or how to treat the infection successfully. So, as with anything unknown, we were all learning to adapt and process new information at a rapid pace. To say this was exhausting is an understatement. Add all of this to the shortages of disinfectants, food and paper products, it felt like we were playing a game of *Whack a Mole* every day.

During times of stress and crisis, the best things we can do are communicate with God and those around us. Asking questions and actively listening to your spouse communicates care and love. It lets them know you are engaged and striving to understand their viewpoint and heartfelt concerns. Scott and I were now in the house together, all day every day. We had time to address those issues life and work caused us to push aside and neglect. Issues like being intentional about spending time together, planning date nights, or simply taking time away from the kids. Also, we needed more intimate time together. Undoubtedly, we needed to address the hurts and pent-up frustrations from the past 4 years, as well. Maintaining a marriage under normal circumstances is hard, but in a pandemic, we quickly realized to survive, we needed to find a new rhythm and head space. It is funny what you concentrate on when life shifts suddenly and things that looked certain, no longer are.

We discussed changing what we were doing to spend more time doing the things we loved to do. Were we working to bring joy into our lives or working just to bring home a paycheck? I admit, I was tired of what I was doing. Scott reminded me that one of my goals I always had was to start and run my own business. I started Positive-Sum Communications, LLC years before when I finished my coaching certification, but it had been hard to generate a profit because of life's interruptions. I was either doing something for the kids or supporting Scott. It was time to start thinking about my own exit strategy. After 23 years as a government contractor, I was weary of the same old stuff, different position cycle.

This was my chance to rebrand myself and move my company forward. With no commute, I could restructure my days and push towards my goal. Scott and I worked on my new website and published it within a month. I started writing again which prompted Scott and I to get our thoughts for this book project on paper. The incubator for the project was our daily discussions about what legacy or blueprint we wanted to leave our children. Then God suddenly took us on a new journey.

During the pandemic, I wanted to connect with other couples. Were they going through the same changes and challenges we were? What could we learn from others that could help us in our marriage? I felt God urging us to do some research to prove what we were writing about was relevant. Maybe I needed to prove it to myself.

Scott and I had never participated in any type of Marriage Ministry during our tenure at our previous churches. We were not asked. Also, the timing or structure of the ministry never felt right, until now. We were ready to take the plunge.

After leaving our last church, we attended a Watch Party of a service broadcast of Elevation Church while at the home of a couple in our local area. It aimed at building community. Elevation Church is based out of North Carolina and streams their weekly message online. People who live outside of North Carolina can view the message from anywhere. Before COVID-19 people used to tell me that wasn't *real* church. However, the pandemic created a paradigm shift in how people worship and engage in ministry. Suddenly, this was the new normal and we were all experiencing online or some other form of remote services.

There were a lot of people struggling with this concept but not us, Zoom was a familiar friend and getting to know others through a tiny box was the norm for me. I had been in a Women's eGroup as they are called at our church for years, which is more or less a Bible study group which met online once a week. My leader asked if I would consider leading an eGroup or better yet, they needed married leaders. Scott and I had recently discussed ways we could impact more married couples along with this book, so we knew this was God's way of nudging us forward. We took a leap of faith and signed up for leader training. I had to convince my hesitant husband this would be good for us. What was interesting was Scott and I had worked for the same company, on the same team in our careers, but had never done ministry together.

We had our first online meeting of the *REALationship Matters* marriage eGroup in July 2020. It was one of the biggest blessings of our quarantine period. We had no idea how God would use this group and its leadership team to bless us in ways we could not imagine. I had never felt so supported and appreciated in ministry. God sent so many awesome couples to our group and they showed up consistently every other week for the group. We created a chat to stay in touch with one another daily. Each time we met with our group I became less isolated, more open, and vulnerable. Vulnerability is hard for me, but this group challenges me. I have grown in ways that I could not have grown alone. They make me a better person by making me face myself and the way I react to issues in my marriage. We have couples that have less and those with greater marriage longevity than Scott and I who participate in our eGoup. This is just the type of community we all need to help us face difficult issues like forgiveness, dealing with past hurts, broken dreams, and expectations. It was good to know we were not alone.

Scott and I started not only reimagining our marriage, but also our careers and life. So, in addition to revaluating our financial goals, with all the crazy going on in the world, we decided it was time to do our estate planning. It was one of the things we had put off for a very long time. There were times when we discussed a will, but never contacted anyone to get it done. I think the pandemic brought my own mortality into view. I remember telling the lawyer while completing the paperwork that I had been so busy living; it was hard to think what would happen after I transitioned.

The one thing she brought to my attention was that taking care of this now, is an act of love for my family. I don't want my family to feel confused or in a state of despair because of my negligence in planning for my exit from their lives. I don't wish that on anyone. I have been to many funerals where that was the case. While I understand why people use GoFundMe to pay for funerals, we all need to take responsibility for our own issues and not leave it to our children, families, and the charity of strangers. No one is promised tomorrow. The COVID-19 viral pandemic presented a morbid view last year of how suddenly someone can vanish from our lives, leaving issues of closure, isolation and loneliness that will persist long into the future.

Last year, the holiday season brought back a sense of normalcy. People put-up decorations early, longing for some semblance of joy and an actual reason to celebrate! I love the Christmas holiday season. Last year was extra special because it came with an overwhelming sense of gratitude. Remembering and celebrating the sights and sounds of the season are what always makes the holidays special for our family. We had survived the months long stress and strain of isolation. We were weary, looking forward to a break from the house, and excited about escaping the daily grind.

Winter was upon us; the days were getting shorter and colder. Scott and I decided when my oldest was a toddler that we would take a break from everyone at Christmas and enjoy a vacation with our immediate family. We told both sides of the family not to buy us gifts. We made it known we would only give gifts to the grandparents and Aunt Evelyn, who is like a second mother to us. Honestly, we had no idea the impact of that decision in a season when we could not gather with family for the holidays.

On our holiday vacation, we usually rent a condo or house for a week. We express our joy by baking, singing, watching movies, playing games, reading, and just relaxing. Of course, there is always an escapade or two involved. I love to visit unusual and historical sites everywhere we go. Cece and Lexi have been doing this for so long they research places for us to go. We search for local eateries, cultural icons, and landmarks that make every trip an adventure. It has also given my kids a respect for people who think and experience life differently.

Kids are educated by what we value. Over the years, we have realized the investment of time in our children is more valuable than anything we can buy or give them. As a parent, I am frequently amazed at the way they filter information. It is a little bit different. I gain so much from seeing the world through the eyes of my children. Taking the time to listen to them gives me precious insight which helps me to see them as individuals and celebrate their unique gifts.

A New Year Dawns

YOLANDA

Welcome to 2021. We thought that after 2020, we would be in a better space. It was as if the world believed the pandemic was just going to pack its bags and go back where it came from... no such luck. After the holidays, it was back to work and the exhaustion that came with it. The pause during the holidays only made coming back an unwelcomed reality.

Scott and I had to fight to stay connected and awake. By now Lexi was having mental health issues as remote learning and isolation were taking a toll on her. As a parent I felt helpless and frustrated. I wanted off this merry-go-round of insanity. Between the kids' emotional energy (or lack thereof), managing my home, and coping with the crazy pace at work, I was burning out. I could feel it. This year (2021) is proving to be as unruly and unrelenting as the previous one.

While I was home during the summer of 2020, I picked up a copy of Shonda Rhimes' book, *Year of Yes: How to Dance it Out, Stand in the Sun and Be Your Own Person*. I had no idea this book would be a catalyst of change in my life. Ms. Rhimes talks about how her sister Delores, who called her out one Thanksgiving because she never said "Yes" to anything. Shonda turned it into a challenge. Over the next year she would say yes, even when she wanted to say no. It pushed her out of her comfort zone and empowered her to face her fears. That is exactly what it did for me.

One of my biggest revelations from 2020 was I was too comfortable. I was in a job where I earned a good salary, but I was losing the excitement for what I was doing. I thought about my company and my love for speaking to others in small and large groups. As a certified life coach, one of the tenants I work with clients on is moving forward in purpose. Was I doing this

117

myself? Or, was I allowing the fear of the unknown to keep me in a place where I felt undervalued and underutilized?

Here is where Shonda Rhimes stepped in. On page 79 of her book, she states the following,

> *"You don't have to know. You just have to keep moving forward. You just have to keep doing something, seizing the next opportunity, staying open to trying something new. It doesn't have to fit your vision of the perfect job or the perfect life. Perfect is boring, and dreams are not real. Just... DO."*

I felt God calling me to something new, but I was literally talking myself out of it because I felt scared and not enough. As if she were reading my mind, I get to page 90 of the book and I saw these words,

> *"Who you are today...that's who you are. Be brave. Be amazing. Be worthy. And every single time you get the chance, Stand up in front of people. Let them see you. Speak. Be heard."*

And so, 2021 became my Year of YES.

One of the lessons I learned from the past year is to find beauty in the mess. At the same time, I felt like I was falling apart, God was showing me a new plan for my life. One that would involve me embracing my gifts, talents, and purpose. It was also asking me to walk away from everything I knew and get extremely uncomfortable as I trusted God to lead me to the next iteration of myself. Saying "Yes" led to new opportunities to speak, use my voice to share hope, and free others from mindsets that were holding them back. God had given me this message a couple of years ago based on a scripture, Isaiah 61:1-3 NIV:

118

The Spirit of the Sovereign Lord is on me, because the Lord has anointed me to proclaim good news to the poor. He has sent me to bind up the broken-hearted, to proclaim freedom for the captives and release from darkness for the prisoners, to proclaim the year of the Lord's favor and the day of vengeance of our God, to comfort all who mourn, and provide for those who grieve in Zion—to bestow on them a crown of beauty instead of ashes, the oil of joy instead of mourning, and a garment of praise instead of a spirit of despair. They will be called oaks of righteousness, a planting of the Lord for the display of his splendor.

There is a lot to be processed in this but the pieces I feel responsible for are proclaiming the good news, encouraging people in their faith, celebrating life, and living with joy. I want people to remember that the fires we have all been walking through have not consumed us and God will give us a crown if we give him our pain. He wants to make a trade with you today, give you joy and put a song in your heart. As the old folks used to say, "Trouble don't last always," if you have gotten this far in our book you have witnessed that how you start is not how you have to finish. Life doesn't always give you the best hand. However, if we work with what we have, remember to place everything in the hands of the one who created us, it will become much more than we could ever imagine.

How Does it End?

YOLANDA

Well, I left my job, and I am walking with God daily. I have no idea how this story will end for me. I am closer to God in ways I would have never known had I not walked through the valley of COVID-19. Scott and I are stronger and closer than we have ever been. I have a new level of faith, trust, and discernment in my marriage and my life. I believe God has only begun. He is going to do immeasurably more than we can ask or think. This is my prayer for you, also!

TIME OUT
What foundational issues shaped our quarantine experience?

YOLANDA

God is enough, I am enough, and I have enough. COVID-19 was a test of our dependence on God and interdependence on each other. There were times when we both questioned if what we were doing was enough to protect and provide for our family. As a couple we had to believe that no matter what happened in this pandemic, God would provide for us as long as we trusted in Him and focused on his goodness. He has promised to never leave or forsake us.

Being still has benefits. While Scott and I were in quarantine we had a chance to have conversations about old wounds and unresolved issues that could have caused more friction if we left them to fester. This is a reminder that no matter how long we have been married we need to do regular check-ins with our spouse to make sure we are communicating about issues that matter to them.

SCOTT

God's timing is always perfect! Regardless of our insistence and impatience, God's will and timing will prevail. Many times, during COVID, we were overtaken by feelings of anxiety and fear. We wanted things to go quickly so we could get over them.

It caused us to act irrationally. But once we slowed down and waited on God, we saw his timing was best. God's timing is perfect in all situations in life.

Trust and Surrender. When COVID-19 became a global pandemic, the world as we knew it changed dramatically. New safety measures were instituted and many people lost their lives. When Yolanda and I were sent home from work, we had very little information regarding whether we would be paid, how long we would be in lockdown, and whether or not we would be able to get food and cleaning supplies. We had to trust in the Lord and not lean on our own understanding. We had to learn to surrender and let God take control. This was especially hard for me.

Lesson Sharing

Lesson One: Reflect—Periodically, stop and hit the pause button—Life moves so fast. In our world of hustle and grind sometimes we need to stop and hit the pause button to see if what we are busy doing is good for our marriage and family's well-being. During the pandemic we all had to stop. It was a chance to evaluate how we were living our lives and what we needed to do differently. If tomorrow was your last day on earth, what would you change?

1. Reflect on the past year and breathe.
   a. What are some takeaways?
   b. What was good and what was difficult but helped you grow and develop your character in ways you could not have imagined pre-pandemic?
   c. What were some of your fears and how did you overcome them?
2. What habits did you develop during this pandemic?
   a. Which ones would you continue moving forward?

b. What habits did you stop doing to make room for the new ones?

3. In what one area of your marriage do you need to be more intentional and recommit to? Is it a date night? Writing love notes/texts? Spending quality time?

　　a. Figure out your mate's love languages using Gary Chapmans book or website for the *Five Love Languages* and fill your spouse's love tank.

　　b. Which of your spouse's love languages do you practice regularly, and which need more attention and intention in carrying them out?

　　　Now go ahead, fill each other's love tank.

Lesson Two: Relate—Gratitude will get you through—More is not always better. What if we focused on what God has already given to us? What if we learned to be grateful for some of the things we take for granted, like living another day, the breath in our lungs, and the sun that warms us? Sounds simple but gratitude changes your attitude. People who focus on what is good in their lives tend to be more positive and have better relationships because they know it could all change in a flash.

1. List some things you discovered about your relationship with your spouse, family, and friends during the pandemic that you had not paid attention to before.

　　a. If there are some areas of concern identified, how do you plan to address them?

　　b. Would you be willing to see a counselor for help? Be brave and vulnerable in communicating what you uncover with your spouse.

2. How does remembering the earlier days of your marriage help you in times of crisis? How can you use this to rekindle the love you once felt before those memories started to fade?

3. Gratitude like exercise is increased when we practice it daily.

a. What are some ways that you can express gratitude on a daily basis?

b. What are you grateful for about your spouse?

c. Why not start a gratitude journal or jar to remind you when tough times come what you are grateful for? You can complete it by writing 3 things daily that you are grateful for in your marriage.

Lesson Three: Reveal—Use your faith to keep moving forward—This pandemic has caused levels of anxiety and fear I have not experienced before. Every illusion of control has been shattered, causing many to try and reclaim it by rebelling against mask mandates, social distancing guidelines, and even vaccine hesitancy. But God has not left us. He is still in control of our country, individual lives, and marriages. Proverbs 3:5 gives us a blueprint of what we should do in times of uncertainty: "Trust in the Lord with all your heart and lean not to our own understanding!"

1. Our faith can move us forward even when we don't have all the details.

   a. Where are you waiting on God to give you more information?

   b. Is God waiting on you to move? Trust God to give what you need *as* you go!

2. Is there a purpose or calling that you have been hesitant to work on?

   a. Have you shared your purpose with your spouse and invited them to assist you in growing in this area?

   b. Talk to your spouse. Ask them to work on identifying the purpose of your marriage. Write it down.

   c. How does your lifestyle and activities fit within the marriage purpose? Work and build together. Be a life-long learner and explore something new!

Final Thoughts on
'BLINDSIDED- MARRIAGE IN A PANDEMIC'
Chapter

As we complete the final chapter of this book, we are still in the pandemic. COVID cases are spiking again. There is a new Delta variant currently circulating in the US. This is an unfortunate turn of events just as the country has been loosening restrictions and opening up businesses. We mourn all the lives that have been lost over this past year. This, along with racial tensions, catastrophic weather events, and a contentious election season have left our country devastated and divided. We are going to tear ourselves apart at the seam if we don't start listening and trying to understand one another. Being right can come at a very high price.

Our marriages are no different. When we focus on everything that is wrong in our marriage, we make those things bigger, and we start to belittle the wonderful things our spouse brings to our life. What if we regularly watered our marriage with words of encouragement and compliments? What if we celebrated why we got married monthly? What if we decided to let go of the busy life and embrace what brings us joy instead?

God is still in control no matter what the world looks like. We need to learn to seek Him first in all we do. During uncertain times, seek God to thrive. Yolanda's mom used to always say there are only two things for certain in this world: death and taxes. We would like to add another, change. Change will always be constant. Our response to change within ourselves and in our marriage will determine if we grow apart or closer together during the most turbulent moments when the world crashes in on you. It can be anything: a health crisis, job loss, death, an accident, etc. The unexpected can toss our marriages into chaos if we don't focus on the one that gives us *"a peace that surpasses all understanding."* Philippians 4:7 ESV

"Jesus said, I have told you these things, so that in me you may have peace. In this world you will have trouble. But take heart! I have overcome the world."

John 16:33 NIV

Remember where you have been. Reflect on God's goodness. Rejoice and be grateful for all he has done. Pray for one another and recommit yourself to seeing your marriage as a reflection of God's love for you! We will be praying for you too!

Peace and Blessings!!

Scott and Yolanda

Family Christmas at the Biltmore

REFERENCES

Coelen, C., Detwiler, E., Nuanes, G., & Simpson, A. (Executive Producers). (2014-present). *Married at First Sight* [TV series]. Red Arrow Studios.

The Holy Bible: New International Version. (1983). Hodder and Stoughton. (Original work published 1978)

ESV Study Bible. (2008). Crossway Books.

Cameron, J. (1991). *Terminator 2: Judgment Day* [Film]. Carolco Pictures, Pacific Western, Lightstorm Entertainment, Le Studio Canal+.

Merriam-Webster. (2003). Transition. In Merriam-Webster's collegiate dictionary (11th ed.).

Gray, J. (1992). *Men are from Mars, women are from Venus: A practical guide for improving communication and getting what you want in your relationships.* HarperCollins.

Gray, J. (1996). *Mars and Venus together forever: Relationship skills for lasting love.* HarperPerennial.

Gray, J. (2008). *Why Mars & Venus collide: improving relationships by understanding how men and women cope differently with stress.* HarperCollins.

Shakespeare, W. (2001). Julius Caesar (R. Gill, Ed.; 4th ed.). Oxford University Press.

Franklin, K. (2007). I am God [Song]. On *The Fight of My Life* [Album]. Gospo Centric Records.

Omartian, S. (2014). The power of a praying wife. Harvest House.

Kendrick, A., & Kendrick, S. (2008). *Fireproof* [Film]. Sherwood Pictures.

Rhimes, S. (2016). *Year of yes: How to dance it out, stand in the sun and be your own person.* Simon & Schuster.

BIOGRAPHICAL SKETCHES

Scott Lupton, D.Sc., is a scholar, teacher, speaker, and Information Technology (IT) professional. He has served in church Men's Ministry, Children's Ministry and jointly with his wife of 24 years, Yolanda, in Married Couple's Ministry. Dr. Lupton has been in the IT field for over 25 years. He got his Bachelor of Science degree in Computer Science from Jackson State University, his Master of Science in Engineering degree in Computer Science from Johns Hopkins University, and his Doctor of Science degree in Information Systems and Communications from Robert Morris University. Dr. Lupton is also a proud life member of Kappa Alpha Psi Fraternity, Inc.

Dr. Lupton enjoys fine dining, vacations, and music. He resides in Maryland with Yolanda. They have two daughters, Cecelia and Alexis.

Yolanda Lupton is a speaker, author and transformation strategist. She has been happily married for 24 years to her husband, Scott and they have two beautiful daughters, Cecelia and Alexis. Yolanda is the CEO of Positive-Sum Communications, LLC and the online host of her talk show On the Rise. As a certified personal and executive coach, Yolanda strategizes with people when they are ready to transition from FRUSTRATED to FLOURISHING by showing them how to reach their goals with a plan that aligns with their purpose and LEVERAGES their superpowers! Yolanda does this by utilizing her I.M.A.G.I.N.E program and tapping into the knowledge she has gained from her own journey to live on purpose and with intentionality.

Mrs. Lupton is a graduate of The College of NJ (TCNJ) and a member of Sigma Gamma Rho Sorority, Inc. She enjoys traveling, writing, girl getaway weekends and all things Disney.